D0604549

LIGHTING YOUR HOME

PANTHEON BOOKS 🏛 NEW YORK

TING
YOUR HOME: A PRACTICAL GUIDE

MARY GILLIATT & DOUGLAS BAKER
PHOTOS BY MICHAEL DUNNE & OTHERS
DESIGNED BY JANET ODGIS

GRAPHIC CREDITS

ART DIRECTOR: JANET ODGIS
GRAPHIC DIRECTOR: R. D. SCUDELLARI
ILLUSTRATIONS: ISADORE SELTZER
PRODUCTION DIRECTOR: CONSTANCE MELLON
TYPESETTING & COMPOSITION: THE CLARINDA CO.
PRINTING: THE MURRAY PRINTING CO.
BINDING: THE BOOK PRESS

Copyright © 1979 by Mary Gilliatt and Douglas Baker

All rights reserved under International and Pan-American
Copyright Conventions. Published in the United States
by Pantheon Books, a division of Random House, Inc.,
New York, and simultaneously in Canada by
Random House of Canada Limited, Toronto.

Library of Congress Cataloging in Publication Data
Gilliatt, Mary.
Lighting your home.
Includes index.
1. Lighting.   I. Baker, Douglas, joint
author. II. Title.
TH7703. G54   621.32′2   79-1884
ISBN 0-394-50151-9

The tables on page 163 are reprinted from ASHRAE Standard 90-75,
by permission of the American Society of Heating, Refrigerating,
and Air-Conditioning Engineers, Inc.

Article 400-8 from the 1978 edition of the *National Electrical
Code,* quoted on page 92, is reproduced by permission from
NFPA 70, *National Electrical Code.* Copyright © 1977,
National Fire Protection Association, Boston, Mass.

All photographs were taken by Michael Dunne, except
as otherwise specified. The other photographers are
acknowledged on the pages where their photographs
appear.

Manufactured in the United States of America

First Edition

CONTENTS

ACKNOWLEDGMENTS

We were greatly helped in the preparation of this book by Nancy Evans Christensen of General Electric and her colleagues at Nela Park, Rick Liotta of Lightolier, Janet Turner of Concord Lighting (G.B.), Antonio Morello and Donato Savoie of Morsa, Ralph Bisdale, Victoria and Ronald Borus, and Rex E. Mabe. We are grateful to Mrs. Richard Kelly for giving us permission to use Richard Kelly's evocative descriptions of Ambient Luminescence, Focal Glow, and Play of Brilliants. Our warmest thanks should also go to our editor, Barbara Plumb, and her assistant, Jill Verdick, to designer Janet Odgis, and to publicity director Ann Silber for all their unstinting assistance and enthusiasm, and to Connie Mellon for her always efficient production. Finally, we would thank our respective families for their exceptional patience.

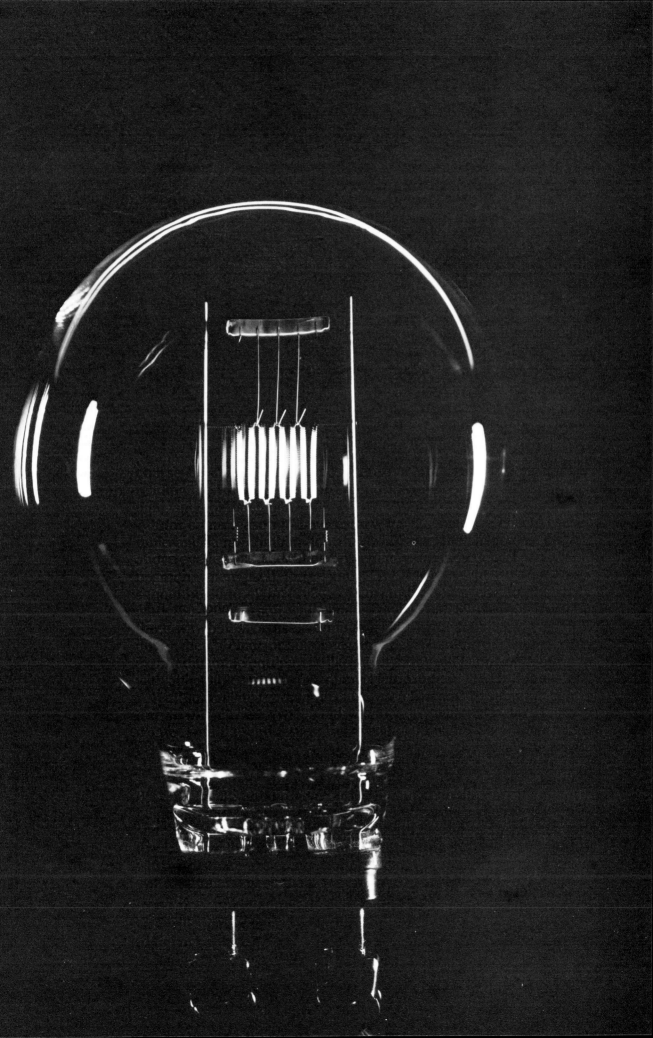

Making the Most of Lighting and This book

In the one hundred years since Edison invented the light bulb—that "hot hairpin in a bottle," as it was graphically described at the time—artificial lighting has made more dramatic progress than any other element in home decoration. From an amazingly carefree alternative to guttering candles, flaring oil lamps, and spluttering gas globes it has developed into a fundamental influence on interior design in particular and architecture and town planning in general. It provides dramatic and often beautiful effects for exteriors—enhancing structure, groupings of buildings, and foliage—and it can add a whole new dimension to casual entertainment, from the sophistications of laser rock to the dazzle that strobe lighting can give to parties.

Artificial light can be made to alter shape and color, to distort or enhance, pick out or flatten, dramatize or minimize, to increase working efficiency, and to form its own subtly changing decoration. Theater designers discovered long ago that the careful control of spots, flood lamps, and colored filters was an instant way to change mood, atmosphere, and feeling on the stage. Museum and art gallery lighting experts know exactly what to do to light a painting, a piece of sculpture, or a precious object to its best advantage. The modification and expansion of these types of lighting for domestic use, together with the wide availability of the dimmer switch, means that people can now not only modify and control light in their own homes but can exaggerate space and texture and pick out possessions or diminish faults at the flick of a switch or the turn of a wrist.

Yet although lighting is one of the most dramatic and important elements in modern design, it is also one of the most confusing, even to people used to the technical sophistication of, say, the latest cooking, laundry, or hi-fi equipment. Most people interested in their home are aware that there are new concepts of lighting which are obviously desirable to put into practice, but they are bewildered by the complexity of the terms used by lighting designers and manufacturers alike. Instead of grasping how to put it all together, too many of us end up bored—or at least confused—by everything to do with the subject.

Take a simple example: people in the trade mean one thing when they use a term like *lamp* (meaning what most of us call a bulb) and the public another (meaning a light fitting that stands on a table or the floor). Whereas *bulb* to the trade means just the glass surround to the filament, the "hot hairpin" of Edison's time. Even so, some manufacturers cater to the public by calling what they would normally term a lamp a bulb in their catalogs. On the other hand, if you are knowledgeable about lighting terms and ask a hardware or grocery store for a lamp, more often than not they will say they do not stock them, when right in front of you is a shelf piled with boxes of bulbs. In this book, which is for the general public and not the cognoscenti, we will call a bulb a bulb and a floor or table lamp a lamp and try not to confuse the issue further.

Preceding page: Photograph by Si Chi Ko of a bare bulb with its glowing filament.

Then too, when most of us think of lighting, we are inclined to think first of all of lights or lamps, the actual fixtures, rather than the sort of effects or moods that can be conjured out of these fixtures, or what the most appropriate light is for a particular space or a specific need. When we buy fixtures we very often buy them for their shape or color or price, but we neglect to find out the sort of light they give—which in any case is difficult to judge in a store full of a hundred different varieties canceling each other out. Even when we know a modicum about the subject and are searching out fixtures to provide interesting background and accent lighting for a room—the spots and wall-washers, downlights and uplights and framing projectors—we all too often buy for looks rather than first making sure what those looks will achieve.

Alternatively, if we do know exactly the sort of effects we want, we may well be foiled by finding that we don't have enough space between floors for the installation of any sort of recessed lighting; or that the entire building is made from impenetrable reinforced concrete which prohibits any attempt to inset fixtures. We might live in rentals where any tampering with walls or ceilings is either impractical or forbidden. Most commonly of all, we might discover that in any event it seems impossible to afford the sort of lighting we would like.

All in all, the workings of electricity remain something of an enigma to most people. Because our reactions to light are often purely sensual and not consciously learned, we are more often than not only grateful that electricity and light just happen. We are happy that it is possible to see in the dark without being fussy about the kind, quantity, and quality of light that might be best, how and where light should fall for various tasks, or the gradations of light that could make all the difference to a room. Using light well, and having light, is not unlike the difference between enjoying the delicate variations of superb cooking and just filling up with food.

To help sort out some of this confusion, and before going on to describe all the ways of using light to its best advantage, we have devised a section of answers to the most commonly asked questions. This, together with an alphabetical glossary or lighting vocabulary at the back of the book, should help to clarify the subject from the start and provide a key to the technical terms that inevitably slip into any explanations about lighting.

On close inspection it will be obvious that parts of the book are repetitive, but this is done on purpose so that readers can look up any particular point at any one time and hopefully find it helpful for their particular query. There are sections on what light is best for what purpose, on using available fixtures to their best advantage, and on planning light for specific rooms. There are chapters on decorating with light, lighting art and objects, lighting indoor plants, and outdoor lighting. And for the more handy and technical-minded there is a section on do-it-yourself ideas. The text, which has been kept as simple and free from jargon as possible, is illustrated wherever illustrations make points more understandable.

SOME COMMON QUESTIONS & ANSWERS

Some Common Questions and Answers

The word lighting almost automatically raises questions that a good many people might like to get clear before studying the subject in greater detail. This section is intended as a quick guide to the sort of queries that are most commonly raised, and aims right from the start to give an elementary working knowledge about different types of lighting terms and their proper use.

It can be used on its own as a basic primer or as a preliminary guide to points treated more fully in appropriate places elsewhere in the book. Some of the terms are also explained in the alphabetical glossary of technical terms at the end—not to be boringly repetitive but rather to keep continuity and to ensure that reference areas are as complete as necessary.

What is the difference between incandescent or tungsten light and fluorescent light? An incandescent bulb produces light when its filament (which is made of tungsten) is heated to a given temperature by the passage of electricity. It gives a pleasant golden light and is therefore much more favored domestically than the more efficient, cheaper to run, and energy-saving fluorescent variety, which is usually colder to look at.

Fluorescent bulbs are tubular in shape and coated on the inside with phosphors. Their light is produced when the phosphors transform ultraviolet energy generated by a low-pressure electric discharge through mercury vapor. There are many different kinds of "white" fluorescent lamps, but the most satisfactory color is given by the Westinghouse Ultralume 3000 bulb, which enlivens all colors tremendously. Unfortunately, at present this is expensive, as well as quite hard to get. The next best is "warm white de luxe." With normal domestic use and cleaning care, fluorescent bulbs will last 6 to 8 years.

What is AC and what is DC? AC (or alternating current) is a flow of electricity which periodically changes its direction. In the U.S., and in most of the world, in fact, this change in direction takes place 60 times each second, but in the U.K. it takes place 50 times each second.

DC (or direct current) means electricity flowing in a given direction. Incandescent bulbs work equally well with DC or AC, but most fluorescent or H.I.D. bulbs work only on AC and need ballasts which act as stabilizing influences in order to operate. Electricity from a battery is DC, but otherwise one rarely comes across it.

What are H.I.D. bulbs, then? H.I.D. stands for "high intensity discharge"; a discharge bulb is any bulb in which light is produced by the passage of an electric current through a vapor or gas. As we have already mentioned, fluorescent bulbs pass a current through mercury vapor, so fluorescents belong to the discharge family. H.I.D. bulbs have a small, bright light source, and some produce light by means of a fluorescing coating on the bulb.

Preceding pages: Surface-mounted framing projectors, 36 in./91 cm from the wall, provide "paintings" of pure light. (One is off, one is aimed at the cushion below.) The uplight on the left casts a soft glow over the center of the room which manages to look gentle and dramatic at the same time. Interior design by Forbes-Ergas Design Associates, lighting design by Douglas Baker. Photo by Norman McGrath

Top right: Sketch of a silvered-bowl bulb. The silver or aluminum reflector coating directs light as needed.

Center right: A typical R bulb.

Bottom right: A PAR 38 bulb. The beam of light from R or PAR bulbs can be wide (flood) or narrow (spot).

What is a transformer? A transformer is an instrument that allows the input of one voltage and the output of another.

What does voltage mean? Voltage is the potential energy available in an electrical circuit—rather like the pressure in a water-supply system. You must not use appliances stating that they use a higher or lower voltage than the circuit available without a transformer, and in the same way it is almost always necessary to use a transformer with any light fixture or appliance bought in another country.

What are amps? Amps are units in electricity used to measure the amount of electric current flowing through a conductor.

What are watts or wattage? Watts or wattage means the amount of power being delivered as a result of the flow of a current (amps) multiplied by the pressure of that flow (volts). All bulbs, appliances, and devices such as plugs and outlets are marked with number of volts and amps, indicating allowable limits.

What do people mean by low-voltage bulbs? Low-voltage PAR bulbs are only 12 volts and have a very precise beam that is useful for pinpoint lighting. When they are connected to a normal voltage line they must be operated on a transformer. They come in spot and flood forms, and some of them are specially designed to cast a rectangular beam for highlighting objects.

What is the difference between a flood and a spot bulb? A flood produces a wide beam (or flood) of light, while a spot bulb produces a narrow beam. The exact spread of each is best determined by looking at examples in action.

What is a reflector bulb? Reflector bulbs are incandescent bulbs with a silver or aluminum reflector coating to direct light where needed. The projected beam can be wide or narrow, as in a flood or spot bulb; to make every watt count you could replace all regular 100 w. bulbs in directional fixtures or task lamps with 50 w. R20 reflector bulbs (60 w. in U.K.). Amazingly, you will get the same amount of light on the task for less running cost.

What does lumen mean? A lumen is the technical term for a unit of light quantity. Just as the performance of a car is measured in horsepower, so light is measured in candlepower, or as they say nowadays, candelas. But one standard candle produces about 12½ lumens; a new 75 w. incandescent bulb, 1,180 lumens; and a new 40 w. warm-white fluorescent bulb, 3,150 lumens. Put like this, you can see why fluorescent light is more economical.

Why do bulbs go dark after a while? As the tungsten filament inside an incandescent bulb emits light, molecules of the metal "boil off." They are carried by the hot gases circulating within the bulb to the top of the bulb where they are deposited on the cooler bulb surface, causing the whole thing to blacken. This is why bulbs that have burned for a long time are much darker than new bulbs. Darkened bulbs, of course, give less light than their rated output while using the same amount of power, or watts; for most efficient use of energy, darkened bulbs should be replaced before they burn out altogether.

Why do bulbs burn out or just "pop"?   Eventually, so much tungsten boils away that the filament breaks and the bulb "burns" itself out. If the filament is designed to burn at a very high temperature, it will glow very brightly, but the tungsten will vaporize quickly and the bulb life will be very short. That is why a photoflood bulb can produce an amazing amount of light, but only for a very short time.

On the other hand, if the filament of a bulb is designed to burn at a relatively low temperature, it will not glow as brightly but will last longer because the tungsten boils away more slowly.

How long should a household bulb last on average?   The average life of a household bulb ranges from 750 to 1,000 hours.

Is there any snag about "long-life" bulbs?   Long-life bulbs are not a particularly good investment in these days of energy conservation. They do last a very long while—up to 2,500 hours or more—but only at the cost of low efficiency, or much waste of energy.

What is a wallwasher?   A wallwasher is a light fixture that when installed the correct distance away from a wall, usually 3 ft./.9 m, will light it evenly from top to bottom, or vice versa, without spilling or wasting light away from the wall into the room. Angled closer to a wall of paintings or a mixture of art, wallwashers will splash light onto varying surfaces, leaving contrasting shadows in between. Or they will simply make a color more brilliant or a molding more effective.

What is a downlight?   Downlights are just that: round or square metal canisters that can be recessed into a ceiling, semi-recessed, or ceiling-mounted to cast pools of light on the floor or any surface below them. Some of them need a 9 to 11 in. (23–28 cm) recess, a few just under 6 in./15 cm. The kind of pool of light depends on whether the bulb inside is a spot, a floodlight, or an ordinary bulb. A spot will throw a concentrated circle of light, a floodlight will give a wider, less intense, cone-shaped light, and an ordinary bulb will provide soft, all-over lighting. Most downlights are fitted with some sort of anti-glare device, and some of them are baffled to give a directional light. Some can be used for wallwashing, and some for pinpointing. Wallwashing means literally bathing a wall with light, which will usually expand the feeling of space.

Above: Cutaway view of cornice used to hide surface-mounted fixtures (which could be fluorescent or, preferably, incandescent reflector bulbs) to wash the wall below with light as well as give an even distribution over pictures.

Top right: Light spills from well-placed wallwashers through a curved landing aperture and onto the alcove below in lighting designer Luciano Zucchi's house in London. Fixtures are invisible; the only indications of their existence are the dimmer switch and conventional switches on the wall at left.

Bottom left: Track-mounted wallwashers by Lightolier, with cutaway canister shape.

Bottom center: Typical ceiling-recessed wallwasher, also by Lightolier.

Bottom right: A Lightolier ceiling-recessed framing projector which can be adjusted to precisely "frame" a surface, whether a picture or a tabletop.

Left: A single downlight provides "Focal Glow" (see page 31) over a round dining table.

Center top: A floor wallwasher by Lightolier which can be plugged in anywhere.

Center bottom: A Lightolier uplight, which must be one of the most useful lights of all since it can be placed behind almost anything to give concealed light.

Bottom right: This shows the wide angle of light from an uplight fitted with a PAR 38 flood bulb (a spot would give a narrower beam).

What is an uplight? Uplights are downlights in reverse in different diameters holding various intensities of bulbs. They are also extraordinarily versatile and a godsend to people living in rentals, or without ceiling recesses or the possibility of recessing, who still want to experiment with background light and concealed light sources. Put them on the floor behind sofas or plants, under glass shelves, and in corners, and they will give a beautiful dramatic accent light, bouncing reflected light off ceilings and into the room, creating shadows and moods that could rarely be imagined by day.

What does a dimmer switch do? Dimmer switches give a variety of different light levels at the turn of a knob. There are inexpensive varieties that fit in place of the usual light switch as well as multiple control units that control several circuits from the same point. There are also separate table-lamp dimmers which can equally well be used to control uplights. Contrary to general opinion, they can be operated with fluorescent lights, though a special type is needed and special ballasts must be used. All in all, as well as being an essential ingredient of any sort of flexible or subtle lighting scheme, they save energy, bulb life, and running costs by reducing current consumption.

You hear a lot about track lighting. What is it exactly and how is it best used? Track, as it is called in the trade, makes it possible for one electrical outlet to supply a number of separate fittings that can be fitted at any point along its length. It can be surface-mounted or recessed, used in or on ceilings, on walls, above baseboards or skirtings, and can be fixed vertically or horizontally, singly, in parallel pairs, or in squares, rectangles, or large-diameter circles. It is obviously versatile, and it can be particularly useful—if you do not mind its somewhat technical appearance in a domestic setting (though recessed track *can* look rather elegant)—when there are no ceiling recesses to speak of, or not enough to allow recessed lights; when the ceilings are made of reinforced concrete; or, quite

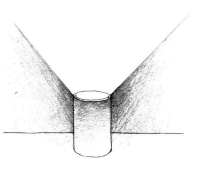

Above: An uplight placed behind a plant in designer Richard Ryan's New York apartment. Note the interesting shadows thrown onto the ceiling by the spiky leaves.

simply, when there are not enough outlets. Lightolier of America now produces a miniature track called Lyte Trim with miniature spots for bookshelves, headboards, and the insides of cupboards, which can be fixed with the twist of a couple of screws by even the most unmechanical-minded person.

What do you do when you have no electrical outlet in the right place and don't want the bother of getting, or can't afford to hire, an electrician?

The first possibility is to consider putting one there yourself. Before you start to feel horrified enough to shut this book in disgust, it *may* not be too difficult if you are handy enough to follow the directions in Chapter 6, "Do-It-Yourself Ideas." But do make sure that the location you are thinking of really is the most useful place. The second possibility is to bring electricity to it from some existing outlet, either by means of a length of track or a length of wire.

If you use flexible cord it can be handled two ways: one is not to try to hide or camouflage it but to drape it from the fixture over to the nearest wall and then down to a receptacle where it is plugged in, in a

Left: Track lighting in this room means that spots can be aimed to light paintings, to reflect light off walls, and to light up table surface and all objects

Bottom left: Paintings lit with wall-washers suspended from a length of track.

Bottom center: Note how you can get exact control of a beam from framing projectors.

Bottom right: Neatly recessed wall-washers flood a wall with even light so that pictures can be rearranged at will.

for-all-to-see, down-to-earth way. The other is to run the wire tight against the ceiling and/or wall and down to the receptacle, trying to disguise it as neatly as you can by seaming it fast to corners where possible and painting it in the relevant places. But you must check whether or not this can be done in your locality and still be within the electrical code requirements. The U.S. National Electrical Code is tough on flexible cords (see page 92).

You could consider a third possibility: to check out an entirely different method of lighting. For instance, you might be thinking of the importance of lighting a particular painting from an adjustable fixture like a spot on the ceiling when it might just as well be lit from a wallwasher set on the floor. Don't forget that uplights and portable floor wallwashers can provide very flexible and purely cosmetic (that is to say, not necessitating anything structural) ways of dealing with art display.

What is the best way to light a painting?   First, it is important to find out if light from any particular direction causes strange things to happen, for instance because of reflections from varnish on the canvas, or on the glass covering, or from some unnoticed quality in the texture of the paint. The best lighting fixture to use on any painting is without doubt a framing projector (see glossary, page 167), which is a light built specifically for such purposes, and which will frame, or light exactly, the area of the painting and no more. But they are expensive—very—and in any case might not be practical or even possible to use.

The next best way is to use a plain flood or spot lamp, from any convenient position—again, if it is possible. But do remember that with either of these two methods the fixture must be located as close as it can be to the painting so that people walk through the beam of light as little as possible.

A wallwasher, either on the floor or ceiling-mounted, can be used also. But remember that while it will probably do a fair job on the painting, it will also light a large part of the wall as well, which you

Above: Paintings can be well lit from below with adjustable uplights.

Left: Two spots are angled onto the large painting, and a recessed downlight centered behind them illuminates the table area. An uplight in the left-hand corner and a table lamp in the right give interesting accent lights. Room design by Ronald and Victoria Borus in conjunction with Ralph Bisdale.

Right: In another space designed by the Boruses, low-voltage spots with pale color filters are aimed through a vase of twigs to cast gently colored shadows on a wall.

Below: When lighting sculpture, objects, or plants, experiment with the light source to see the best angle to use.

may not want—unless, of course, you have a whole wall of prints or drawings that you want illuminated, or small paintings that you are constantly switching and swapping around.

The last and most economical way (but, as economies often prove to be, the least effective) is to use a picture light of the kind that clamps or screws onto the frame of the painting or the wall behind. The defect here is that such a fixture does not throw light very far, or evenly down across the painting. Still, it is far better than nothing (see Chapter 7, "Lighting Art and Objects").

What is the best way to light a piece of sculpture (or an object, a plant, an arrangement of flowers, or whatever)?

Let's start by saying that the worst way is usually from directly overhead, except perhaps in the case of an indoor tree or large plant, when, of course, the source of light must be far enough above not to scorch the leaves. But the best way can only be determined by trial and error. Use a work light (described and explained in Chapter 3, "General Planning") and position it, or have somebody hold it for

you, so that the sculpture or whatever is seen lit from many different angles. If light from one direction produces shadows that make the piece unrecognizable or cause strange reflections or unexpected highlights, that direction is no good. Try another. Nor is it acceptable if the light source is in any way annoying to people in the room. Occasionally, you may need to try light from more than one direction, possibly with a flood from one location and a spot from another.

Generally, light aimed at an angle of about 30 degrees from the vertical is suitable, because it corresponds to our experience with sunlight and because it won't get in people's eyes too much. Given typical 8½ to 9 ft. (2.6–2.75 m) ceiling heights, a 75 w. PAR 38 spot bulb is the first lamp to try on a small object or arrangement (or a 150 w. spot attached to a dimmer). On a larger piece, start experimenting with a 150 w. PAR 38 flood. These PAR (*p*arabolic *a*luminized *r*eflector) bulbs have a punchier, more dramatic light with tighter control of beam spread than an ordinary R-type reflector bulb, and, as with R bulbs, their sealed-in reflectors never need cleaning (see Chapter 7, "Lighting Art and Objects").

What is the ideal position for a lamp when reading? Is it true that it should always be behind the right shoulder?
The best position for a reading light is to the side (left *or* right) of the reading material, so that light is not reflected into your eyes from glossy print or paper. The lower edge of the shade should be at eye level for a seated person, and the center of the base of the lamp should be in line with the shoulder and 20 in./51 cm to the left or right of the center of the book. The idea that the lamp must be on one side or the other is quite without foundation. (For best positions for writing lamps, see Chapter 3, "General Planning.")

Left: Note how adjustable and traditional lamps differ in their degree of control and spread of light. Both are rightly positioned in the drawings to show where the light should fall for the most relaxed reading position.

Right: Hanging lamps on either side of this sofa light plants and end table and give interesting accent light.

You read a lot about mood lighting, but how do you achieve it? High levels of controlled general lighting are usually cheerful and stimulate people to activity. Low levels tend to create an atmosphere of relaxation and intimacy, and a warm intimate atmosphere in a room is established by having small pools of light. These, by their very nature, emphasize a shared center of attraction such as the area where you and someone else are eating, or reading, or pursuing an activity together. The areas illuminated must be limited in size and below eye level, and the fixtures producing these pools of light must be within the actual reach of the people involved.

At the other end of the scale, an impersonal, more detached but stimulating feeling is achieved by putting light onto vertical surfaces such as walls, curtains, or blinds, or by using a relatively large number of light sources throughout the room. One is forced by this to see the room as a whole and to become part of a larger and therefore less personal context. Between these extremes lie many combinations. A little experimenting and careful observation will show you many effects, but it is always more than useful to install dimmer switches to ring any sort of changes and moods in lighting. (See Chapter 3, "General Planning"; Chapter 4, "Room-by-Room Guide"; and Chapter 5, "Decorating with Light and Lights.")

Can you achieve changes in levels of light on table and floor lamps by other means than dimmer switches? Yes. Three-way switches are another way. They are not so subtle, but they do provide three quite different light levels. Three-way switches are a common feature on many American lamps, and three-way bulbs come in a variety of wattages.

GENERAL
PLANNING

General
Planning

When all is said and done—and a lot is always being said and done, not to say written, about lighting, to the often rueful confusion of the general public—domestic lighting can be divided quite simply into three distinct types:

- *General or background lighting*
- *Local or task lighting*
- *Accent or decorative lighting*

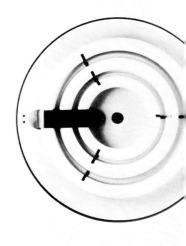

Ideally, every room should be a combination or variation, to a greater or lesser degree depending upon function, of at least two of these types. In living rooms all three types should be used. All of them can be controlled—that is to say, the light level subtly modulated—by simply turning a dimmer switch, which can be installed along with or instead of the ordinary light switches.

GENERAL OR BACKGROUND LIGHTING means maintaining a low level of light throughout the living area for moving about easily and in safety, and for providing the kind of framework that will make local or task and accent lighting both more helpful and more interesting.

This sort of light is usually provided by ceiling fixtures of one sort or another, or even a whole completely engineered luminous ceiling; lighted valances; cove, cornice, or wall lighting (see glossary); recessed fixtures either in ceilings or floors; or a grouping of at least three portable lights, like uplights, set in judicious places at floor level to bounce light off ceilings and walls. Or the same number of lamps can be used, because each lamp will only spread its light over about 40 to 50 sq. ft. (3.7–4.6 sq. m).

LOCAL OR TASK LIGHTING is light of any sort that provides the right level of illumination for a wide range of actions from reading and writing to eating, cooking, sewing, painting, making up, and shaving, as well as creating interesting pools of light.

In living areas it is usually provided by table, desk, or floor lamps; in kitchens and laundry rooms by fixtures like fluorescent strip lights or incandescent strips and/or spots; in bathrooms it could be by installing bulbs all round a mirror, as in theater dressing rooms, as well as downlights over baths and basins.

ACCENT OR DECORATIVE LIGHTING creates focal points, emphasizes paintings, objects, and possessions that you want emphasized, and adds the interesting personal or idiosyncratic touch to a room. The sort of fixtures to use for this sort of highlighting are the various types of spots, wallwashers, pinhole or framing projectors, uplights, and even tiny Christmas-tree lights (which do not have to be confined to Christmas) and candles.

These are the bare bones of lighting, the prosaic underpinnings. But artificial light is after all a substitute for daylight, which is never

Preceding page, left: A still life of bulbs of every shape and size from General Electric.

Preceding page, right: Box-shaped shades from Morsa have a nicely dégagé air and can be used singly on walls or piled on the floor in sculptural shapes.

Top left: A circline fluorescent bulb and fixture (see glossary, page 166) from Morsa.

Center left: A bare G 40 white incandescent bulb and fixture from Atelier International. These look good in their own right and can be used in many situations.

Bottom left: A Morsa light fixture with a tubular incandescent bulb concealed by a long colored and curved baffle lined in white.

Below: This is the useful work lamp described on page 32. It is particularly useful for experimenting with the direction, kind, and placement of light in a room.

Right: These floor and pendant fixtures by Castelli not only throw a pleasant diffuse light but are decorative in their own right.

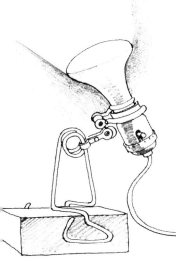

static but always shifting and flowing. It might help to get the *feel* of light as a medium to be used and manipulated, as a painter subtly mixes paint, or a cook experiments with different herbs or spices for a recipe, if one thinks of these three sorts of light in terms of the different moods of daylight and how similar effects can be created: like sun coming through an early mist; sparkle on dew and snow, frost and glass; light glinting off rocky surfaces next to dark crevices; late afternoon mellowness.

Again, there are the images that spring to mind when reading someone like the late Richard Kelly, the American lighting expert, who had his own fancifully described labels for the three kinds of basic lighting, which he melded into one another in his descriptions—just as good lighting methods should meld into each other to form a sometimes dramatic but always harmonious whole. At least some of his images should strike a responsive cord in even the most pragmatic of us, which in turn should trigger off other comparisons, and, hopefully, ideas.

He described our rather prosaic background lighting as "Ambient Luminescence . . . a snowy morning in open country . . . twilight haze on a mountain top or a cloudy day on the ocean. . . . It is the light in a white tent at noon, or in a brilliantly lighted white room without visible light. It is all we sense of indirect lighting. . . . Ambient Luminescence is shadowless illumination. It minimizes form and bulk. It dematerializes . . . it reduces the importance of all things

and all people. It fills people with a sense of freedom of space and can suggest infinity. It is usually reassuring and restful."

Local lighting is Richard Kelly's "Focal Glow. . . . The campfire of all time, the glowing embers around which stories are told, or the football rally bonfire. Focal Glow is the limelight, the follow spot on the stage, an aircraft beacon. . . . It is the light burning at the window or the welcoming gleam of the open door. . . . Focal Glow is the sunburst through the clouds and the shaft of sunshine that warms the far end of the valley . . . it is the pool of light at your favorite reading chair, your airplane seat light . . . matchlight on a face. Focal Glow is the end of the rainbow; it commands attention, creates interest, fixes the gaze, tells people what to look at. Focal Glow separates the important from the unimportant, establishes precedence, can induce movement . . . can control and direct traffic. . . ."

Accent or decorative light is the "Play of Brilliants, the sensation of a cache of diamonds in an opened cave, or the Versailles Hall of Mirrors with its thousands of candle flames . . . a ballroom of crystal chandeliers. Play of Brilliants is Times Square at night . . . sunlight on a tumbling brook . . . the heaven full of stars . . . phosphorous waters in the churning wake of a boat . . . birch trees interlaced by a motor car's headlights. Play of Brilliants excites the optic nerves . . . stimulates the body and spirit and charms the senses. It creates a feeling of aliveness, alerts the mind, awakens curiosity and sharpens the wits. It quickens the appetite . . . heightens all sensations. It can be

Above: Corrugated aluminum walls shine with reflected light from uplights and the television screens in an avant-garde bedroom designed by Richard Ryan for Bloomingdale's. A floor lamp behind the couch can be positioned as required for the most comfortable reading light.

Left: Eyeball spots are placed above the shelf which acts as part of the bed head in this bedroom, and wall lamps placed above and slightly to one side of the pillows give reasonable reading light. Behind the bed wall, a track with angled downlights picks out the large plants.

Right: A mixture of light fixtures in the kitchen-dining area of a Fire Island house. Pendant lights hang over the counter top; recessed downlights cast pools of light on the floor, and the glass table is lit by flickering storm lamps to give the accent or decorative light, as well as a decorative row of suspended incandescent tubes set below the skylight.

distracting or it can be entertaining."

It is not so hard, once these sorts of images have been assimilated and others formulated from them, to get an inkling of the unlimited variations that can be achieved given the right understanding—and so distribution—of light, color, and intensity.

But to create any sort of successful build-up of light and lighting moods one must equally well understand not just the roles played by the various sorts of bulbs and fixtures on the market, and how they best fit into our three main lighting categories, but how much light is comfortable for any given space and purpose.

At the end of this chapter we give a general summary of the light fixtures mentioned under each category, together with points to look for in their design, and where and how they will work best. It might look like an awful lot to wade through at first, but it will save you an enormous amount of time—and disappointment in the eventual effect—if you study it carefully before any actual purchase.

In the meantime, though, you will also have to decide on the direction, kind, and placing of light that will suit your way of life, room shapes, and possessions. A most useful piece of equipment to invest in at this point would be a work lamp like the one illustrated at the bottom of page 29: a socket with a swiveling spring clamp that will be useful for testing quality, quantity, and direction of light as well as in innumerable daily situations. You can clamp it onto the leg of a chair, a door, an overhead joist, a brick, or a piece of wood on the floor and generally experiment with it to determine what sort of light looks best, where it should come from to hit the right spot, and what different kinds of bulbs and wattages will work best for your particular needs and tastes.

Buy a 150 w. PAR 38 flood bulb to use in this experimental stage, and make your experiments doubly useful by controlling the amount of light with an inexpensive dimmer. A dimmer with a 600 w. capacity is generally available quite inexpensively, and it can always be connected to a table or floor lamp.

Far left: In Doreen Chu's Manhattan apartment, vertical aluminum louvered blinds reflect back light from the floor lamps positioned behind the sofa. Polished aluminum ceiling tiles (not seen) over the dining table are inset with bare bulbs to give sparkle and visually expand space and light at the same time. The combination of white walls and grey carpet with the shine of glass and aluminum pepped up by clever lighting is unexpectedly vivacious in a low-key scheme.

Center: A mirrored ceiling panel inset with small white bulbs gives sparkle, reflection, and interest. The fixture is by Lightolier and commercially available.

Right: Ceiling-mounted downlights graze the curtains and give soft background light. An uplight to one side of the chimney embrasure casts a glow on the brick wall. The indoor tree is strung with lights like a Christmas tree to give the "Play of Brilliants" described on page 31. Photograph by Robert Perron.

Page 34: In this London sitting room most of the light is from uplights concealed behind the skirted tables and plant baskets and in corners. Small recessed wallwashers allow maximum flexibility with paintings and drawings and produce a scalloped effect on the glazed walls. The level of all light is controlled by a series of dimmer switches. Designed by Mary Gilliatt.

Page 35, top: This brick-walled London kitchen is lit by strip lights over the counter tops (not seen), two spots on dimmers recessed into the frame of the skylight above the hanging plants and table, and uplights placed in the corners to graze the walls with light and at the same time exaggerate their texture. The Victorian Gothic glass-framed bookcase, now holding glass and china, is lit by concealed strip lights at the sides of the shelves inside the glass doors. A further strip light concealed on top of the bookcase shows off the old Dutch plate and part of the tongue-and-grooved wood ceiling. Designed by Mary Gilliatt. Architect Nicholas Hills.

Page 35, bottom: Firelight and the modern glass oil lamps add to the light concealed behind the Gothic bench to give a gentle glow in another view of the same London kitchen.

Top left: Uplights and firelight are the main sources of light in this London hall-library with a wall-mounted spot angled on the far bookcase to give an extra boost when necessary. A wall-mounted downlight set a couple of feet above the door in the lower-level lobby gives an extra glow against the gloss of the darker walls. The uplights are concealed behind the late-nineteenth-century chairs and the cloisonnée table. Designed by Mary Gilliatt. Architect Nicholas Hills.

Bottom left: In Cecil Beaton's country house in England, lamplight spills over a table of flowers and memorabilia, creating just the "Focal Glow" talked about by Richard Kelly on page 31.

Bottom center: More "Focal Glow" in this powder room where the tall, slim lamps at either side of the wash-basin give quite enough light for a quick touch-up.

Bottom right: Swivel-armed brass lamps on either side of the mirror throw light on the face and also fit in with the feeling of this Edwardian-looking bath-room in London. Designed by Nicholas Hills.

SUMMARY OF LIGHT FIXTURES
TO USE FOR GENERAL OR BACKGROUND LIGHT

Surface-mounted or suspended ceiling fixtures   These are
better shaded by completely diffusing materials like opal or ceramic
enameled glass, diffusing plastic, or paper, as in Japanese shades. The
larger the diameter of the enclosure, the lower its brightness and the
softer the shadows cast by it.

Ceiling-mounted lights   Ceiling-mounted lights in living areas
come readily into the line of sight and should therefore have only half
the surface brightness of similar lights in utility areas like kitchens,
laundry rooms, and bathrooms, where the task is more important
than the ambience.

A well-shaded light distributing light up, down, and to the sides will
create a much more restful atmosphere in a room than one that produces only downward light, which can make the person right underneath feel as though picked out by an obtrusive spotlight.

If using downlights proper, which do have the advantage of being
reasonably unobtrusive if well placed, use fixtures providing a wide
rather than a narrow beam of light and locate them more toward the
side of a room than in the center above the normal flow of movement.
If they are the main source of general lighting there should always be
several per room. If there is only one outlet, recessed or surface-

r left: Rows of white bulbs on
mmer switches provide very pleasant
neral and task light in this New York
chen. Another row lights shelves.

ft: This canvas-and-wood fixture
th its levers and pulleys is an updated
rsion of the familiar rise-and-fall
np, and gives a pleasant diffused light
well as being a decorative object in
own right. It takes a small spot bulb
d comes from Morsa.

low left: The pendant lamp sus-
nded over the desk in the sketch
es the surface from extra clutter as
ll as giving excellent overall light.

low right: A chandelier fitting over
s table is supplemented by a down-
ht to combine the decorative with
e practical. (See text on right.)

mounted track can be used with several lights on one track.

Lights suspended from the ceiling Remember that lights suspended from the ceiling that reflect all or nearly all of their light back onto the ceiling for redistribution produce comfortable but bland general lighting. This needs to be controlled with a dimmer, if possible, and can be pepped up by accent lighting.

Chandeliers, candelabra, or old lanterns These should never be depended upon exclusively for their light. The effect—however beautiful the fitting—will be one of dull flatness and lack of variety. There are two reasons for this:

1. Whenever you are in a space, unless you are facing the wall closest to you, the center light is within your field of view; since it cannot be avoided or ignored, it becomes a dominant factor regardless of whether, on aesthetic grounds, it deserves to be.

2. It is a completely unnatural light. We are used to seeing our entire daylight environment lit at any given time from one direction (that is, from the sun). But with a lone central fixture everything seems to be lit nondirectionally with no familiar patterns of highlights and shadows.

Therefore, this sort of lighting fixtures should be supplemented by recessed downlights or table lamps and uplights wherever possible.

Recessed fixtures Since any recessed fitting has to be installed in the ceiling, a certain amount of preplanning is necessary. Is the space between the ceiling and the floor above deep enough to take recessed fixtures? You will need to find out both the depth of recess available to you and the depth that is needed to take them comfortably before attempting to install these fixtures.

Is any permission required from a landlord before they can be installed?

Does the construction of the building, say in concrete, make the project impossible?

Even if these questions can be answered satisfactorily, it is still important to use these sorts of lights in conjunction with a dimmer switch or switches, for as incandescent lights are dimmed, the quality of their light becomes more mellow, gradually changing the atmosphere of the room.

One final question: Are the ceilings so high that you will have to call in an electrician every time a bulb goes? If they are, forget the idea. The nuisance is hardly worth the pleasure of having near-concealed lighting.

If there don't seem to be any difficulties of this sort, think about the various merits and qualities of the different fittings.

If, for example, you want to emphasize a wall texture or treatment, consider the kind of *recessed downlights known as "high-hats."* When they are installed within 6 to 8 in. (15–20 cm) of the relevant wall they will graze it with light in such a way as to exaggerate every nuance. Depending on how far apart they are fixed, they will also produce a pattern of scalloped light and shade that can be very dramatic. Lighting results will of course vary with bulb type, wattage, and fixture design, so it is important to consult the different catalogs and manufacturers' data. But high-hats can usually take any reflector bulbs from 50 to 150 watts.

If, on the other hand, you want a completely smooth wall, consider either *recessed or surface-mounted wallwashers*. Their sort of light does not emphasize texture or variations on a wall surface as do high-hats, since a contoured inner reflector directs a wide spread of nearly uniform light from ceiling to floor, without the scalloped pattern identified with the high-hat downlights. The wall reflects light into the room and gives a relaxed and pleasing atmosphere. For best results they should be spaced about 30 to 36 in. (76–91 cm) from the wall and about the same distance apart, and used in conjuction with 150 w. reflector floodlights.

A more dramatic feeling can be given to a room by using *adjustable downlights*. Use similar reflector bulbs, but mount the fixtures away from the walls and aimed straight down. Again, it is important to use these lights with dimmers to allow changes in the light level; for best effect use a neutral-colored floor covering with a reflectance of 25 percent or higher. Avoid placing units directly above seating areas or the poor sitters might feel that they are being grilled. For the most comfortable effect use one 75 w. reflector floodlight for every 25 sq. ft./2.3 sq. m of floor area.

NONADJUSTABLE DOWNLIGHTS are best suited to utility areas, workshops, and recreation rooms meant for active games. Fixtures can be incandescent or fluorescent.

To avoid glare on the ceiling, choose equipment with one of the following (listed in order from lowest to highest brightness):

1. *Special low-brightness louvers*
   (in the form of specular parabolic wedges)

2. *Reflector for control of light direction*

3. *Metal or plastic louvers*

4. *Lenses for control of light direction*

5. *Flat opal glass, level with ceiling line*

Luminous ceilings Translucent ceilings—consisting of a diffusing material with lighting fixtures above it—will cast light from practically all directions. The effect is rather like an overcast sky, lacking highlights and shadows; this can be peaceful and restful or monotonous, depending on your mood. They are appropriate in bathrooms, kitchens, and possibly hallways and foyers, and the translucent mate-

rial itself can be to some degree decorative, since you can get it in a shaped or molded three-dimensional form, or you can have it painted or colored.

One precaution: An overall translucent ceiling can look as glum and depressing as the sky before a storm unless it is reasonably bright.

Lighted valances, cornices, and wall lights On the whole these can be achieved satisfactorily with both incandescent and fluorescent lighting, but since in the case of cornice and valance lighting (see glossary) the actual bulbs are hidden behind a baffle of some sort, fluorescent has a distinct edge, giving as it does three times as much light as incandescent for the same wattage, quite apart from lasting so much longer. But always use the Westinghouse Ultralume 3000 or the General Electric "warm white de luxe" or "cool white de luxe" for the best color renderings. The Ultralume and the "warm white de luxe" have an effect similar to incandescent light but bring the cooler colors out better (which tend to be slightly greyed down by incandescent). "Cool white de luxe" is especially good for bringing out cool colors, as its name implies, but is best in a hot climate. A third choice could be the newish General Electric Bright Stik, which is a reasonably effective color and convenient because it is so easy to install.

VALANCE LIGHTING is good for curtained windows since it lights both upward and downward. In any case, a valance is traditionally a heading for curtains and when lit it restores the daytime balance to rooms. Upward lighting has the bonus of being fairly informal, and creates a feeling of spaciousness as well as providing subtle general lighting for family rooms, dining areas, and bedrooms. The downward lighting highlights the curtain fabric, often making it look more sumptuous and interesting.

ft: Wallwashers graze the wall with ht, light the painting, bench, and nt, and give light to the whole room well in this particular sketch.

ght: Cornice lighting at the far end the room in this sketch and valance hting above the curtains and pictures e an even wash of light.

erleaf, left: Close-up of Light-er's miniature Lyte Trim track, show-the small spot fixture that clips in.

erleaf, right: Total flexibility: a ivel socket on a taut cable works as a wnlight (top) and as an uplight ottom). From Atelier International.

CORNICE OR COVE LIGHTING provides good general downlight as well as lighting up papered, paneled, painted, and fabric-covered walls, or walls lined with bookshelves, for that matter. It is as acceptable in a traditional as in a modern interior, makes a subtle background for dining, and balances light from portable lamps in living rooms. When used on inside walls, it can balance lighting at windows as well.

WALL LIGHTS give both upward and downward lighting in general, and can be used in the following ways:

- *In family and recreation rooms where portable lamps might get in the way of activities*
- *On staircase walls and landings where they light up and down and are therefore sensible in an accident-prone area*
- *In low-ceilinged rooms where ceiling fixtures might seem to be crowding the space*
- *In rooms that are only wired at the walls*

The table opposite shows the minimum general lighting needed for various room types and sizes, using the sort of background lighting outlined above.

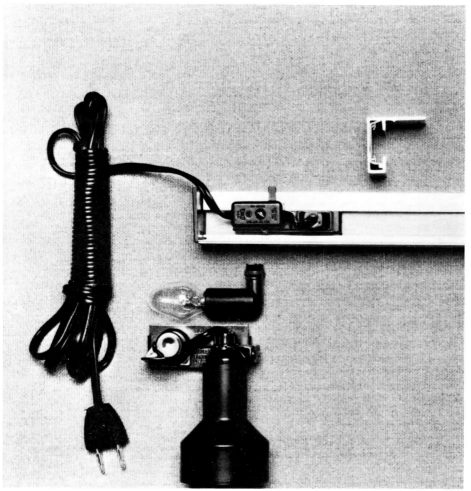

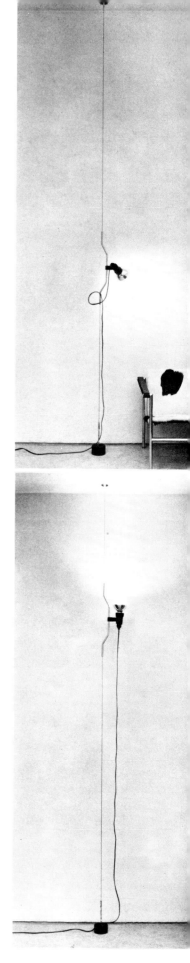

MINIMUM GENERAL OR BACKGROUND LIGHTING NEEDED FOR VARIOUS ROOMS

General living areas:	ceiling-mounted or suspended fixtures	valance or cornice lighting; wall brackets	recessed adjustable lights	recessed nonadjustable lights
Small living rooms, family rooms, bedrooms (i.e. under 150 sq.ft./114 sq.m)	3–5 socket fixtures totaling 150–200 w.	Runs of 8–12 ft. (2.4–3.6 m)	4 50 w. reflector bulbs	4 75 w. incandescent bulbs 2 40 w. fluorescent bulbs (for recreation or family rooms only) in square or rectangular recessed boxes
Average living rooms, family rooms, bedrooms (i.e. 185–250 sq.ft./17–23 sq.m)	fixtures totaling 200–300 w.	Runs of 16–20 ft. (4.8–6 m)	5–8 75 w. reflector bulbs	4 100 w. incandescent bulbs (with minimum size of fixture or fitting: 10, 12, or 14 in./ 25, 30, or 35 cm) 3 40 w. or 4 30 w. fluorescent bulbs
Large rooms (over 250 sq. ft./23 sq.m)	1 watt per sq.ft./93 sq.cm) and 1 fixture per sq.ft./11.6 sq.m.	1 ft. per 15 sq.ft.	1 75 w. reflector bulb for each 25 sq.ft./2.3 sq.m.	1 100 w. incandescent or 1 50 w. per 40–50 sq. ft. (3.7–4.6 sq. m) (with minimum size as above) 2 40 w., 3 30 w., or 6 20 w. fluorescent per 100 sq. ft./ 9.3 sq. m
Utility & service rooms: small kitchen, laundry, workshop, bathrooms, washrooms, etc. (i.e. under 75 sq.ft./7 sq.m) (See table in Chapter 10, "Some Energy-Saving Ideas")	150 w. incandescent or total 60 w. fluorescent	Use single run of fluorescents on top of open-to-ceiling cabinets; or in soffit extended 8–12 in. (20–30 cm) beyond cabinets	Not suitable for general lighting in these areas	1 150 w. incandescent bulb (minimum sizes as above) or 2 40 w. fluorescent bulbs
Average (75–120 sq.ft./ 7–11 sq.m)	150–200 w. incandescent or 60–80 w. fluorescent	As above	Not suitable	4 100 w. incandescent or 2 40 w. fluorescent bulbs
Large (over 120 sq.ft./11 sq.m)	2 w. per sq.ft./93 sq.cm of incandescent or ³/₄–1 w. per sq.ft. fluorescent	5–10 w. per sq. ft. in fluorescent for a luminous ceiling (a rather expensive solution)	Not suitable	1 100 w. incandescent per 30 sq. ft./2.8 sq. m or 1 150 w. per 40 sq. ft./3.7 sq. m 2 40 w., 3 30 w., or 6 20 w. fluorescent per 60 sq. ft./ 5.6 sq. m

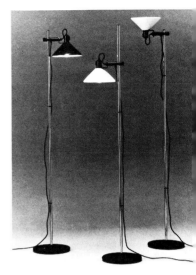

SUMMARY OF LIGHT FIXTURES
FOR LOCAL OR TASK-LIGHTING GROUP

The most useful kind of lighting for this group is given by *portable lamps,* but they really ought to fulfill the following conditions for maximum efficiency. Occasionally, of course, wall and ceiling fixtures are used as well.

In living rooms Table and floor lamps should be both functional and good-looking, providing a generous light for any tasks as well as adding a comfortable feeling to the room.

The total height from floor to lower edge of shade (including table height) should equal eye height from floor (i.e. 38 to 42 in. [97–107 cm] when seated on an easy chair).

Choose three-way or regular soft-white bulbs with a minimum of 150 w. for reading. The three-way variety is preferable because this can be turned on low when not needed for reading. Alternatively, a table-lamp dimmer can be fitted to vary the levels.

An open-top shade is best, with a minimum bottom dimension of 16 in./41 cm. Shallower shades need a louver or shield on top.

Shade materials vary according to the function of the lamp and the decoration of the room. *For reading* it is better to have moderately translucent material like silk or white vinyl parchment laminated to fabric, or white-lined fabric if fairly dense. Only use dense or opaque shades if walls are very dark, and keep in mind that all shades in a room should be similar in brightness.

Avoid strong or dark colors on the outside of shades unless the material is opaque; and the inside should always be white or near white—never shiny. Colored linings tint the light, which can of

Far left: Uplights set in the corners o Richard Ryan's Manhattan apartment cast interesting shadows from urn and plants. A brass floor lamp behind the couch can be moved into the most comfortable position for reading at any given time. An uplight is concealed behind the screen, and the light it casts on the wall is reflected in the mirror opposite, which completely surrounds the fireplace for extra depth and sparkle.

Above: The reversible shade on this floor lamp by Morsa means that light can be thrown up or down, making it a useful and versatile fixture.

Right: Downlights are recessed into the ceiling down the corridor area in Barbara Littman's New Jersey bedroom. They cast a pleasant light on the vertical louvered blind at the far end of the room. Floor lamps on either side of the bed can be adjusted for reading.

Far right: Table lamps on either side of the dressing table light the face in this bedroom designed by Victoria and Ronald Borus. Angled downlights (not seen) light the curtains and bring out the texture of the lace dressing-table cover.

course be splendid for atmosphere but not nearly so splendid for reading. Foil linings are not a good idea since they reflect a harsh light, and not much of it.

If for some reason it is necessary, for a decorative effect, to use a table and lamp combination that will bring the shade substantially above eye level, place the lamp behind your shoulder in a floor-lamp position when used for reading. The base height of *floor lamps* should be 40 to 49 in. (102–124 cm) to the lower edge of the shade, with 150–200 w. soft-white bulbs, or 50/200/250 or 100/200/300 w. three-way bulbs, or use a dimmer switch). This obviously cannot be done when a chair or sofa is against a wall, so for this situation use extra-adjustable equipment like swing-arm wall lamps or floor lamps with adjustable spots with a dimmer attachment.

Wall lamps for reading are also useful in small rooms with furniture that is close to walls and windows, or where a pair of lamps is wanted and the end tables are of unequal height. Good bulbs would be 100–150 w.

In bedrooms

BEDSIDE LAMPS should give both eye and general comfort. The base height should be in line with the shoulder, and when you are in a semi-reclining position the lower edge of the shade should be at eye level. The bulbs should be the same as in living-room table lamps, with a distinct preference for the three-way variety or a dimmer switch attachment so that a partner need not be disturbed.

EXTENDED-ARM WALL LAMPS or fixtures centered two feet from the wall will span wide headboards or side curtains on beds to bring light to the right place.

ar left top: Swing-arm wall lamps
entered slightly in for the most com-
rtable reading light, an uplight to light
e plant and a classic floor lamp for
mchair reading in Dr. Shirley Wray's
ambridge bedroom.

ar left bottom: Picture lights with
candescent strips for reading in bed
a room designed by Ronald and
ctoria Borus.

eft top: Tall bedside lamps and
aglepoise lamps at either side of the
indow seat in another bedroom in
r. Wray's home.

eft bottom: A close-up of the swing-
m wall lamps set above the bed in
r. Wray's bedroom. Note the patterned
aing of the tweed bed curtains. Ward-
be lighting is from a fluorescent strip
oncealed at the top of the closet.

ight: Individually controlled fixtures
a track are an alternative lighting
ethod but should be attached to a
mmer switch to avoid all glare.

ar right: A full-width fluorescent
all bracket gives even light on the
llow area.

verleaf: Daylight pours down from
skylight above the bed in this
merican bedroom and filters through
e shutters. At night, a similar effect is
hieved with carefully placed wall-
ashers. Photograph by Robert Perron.

FLUORESCENT WALL BRACKETS can be good for reading in bed, as they give equally good lighting over the entire width of the bed, allowing much more freedom of movement as well as neatly unifying an arrangement of twin beds and bedside tables or chests. They should be shielded with opaque or semi-translucent material, and mounted so that the lower edge of the faceboard will be 30 in./76 cm above the mattress.

On a single bed use one 36 in. "warm white de luxe" tube. On a double bed use one 48 in. 40 w. "warm white de luxe" tube. On a king-size bed, or across twin beds, use two 36 in./900 mm or two 48 in./1,200 mm tubes.

Ideally, it takes two lamps or pendant fixtures to apply makeup evenly at a bedroom dressing table or dresser. (Alternative lighting is dealt with in Chapter 4, "Room-by-Room Guide.") If you are going to use table lamps, the base heights should be such that shade centers are approximately 22 in./56 cm above a 36 in./91 cm high dresser, or 15 in./38 cm above a 30 in./76 cm dressing table. In any case, the center of the shades should be at cheek height when standing at a dresser or sitting at a dressing table.

Shades should be of highly translucent fiberglass, acetate, plastic, or silk, but should not be highly colored because this will distort the complexion color.

The minimum dimensions should be:

- *Top: 7 in./18 cm*
- *Depth: 7 in./18 cm-plus preferred*
- *Base: 9 to 11 in. (23–28 cm)*

Bulbs should be 30/70/100 w. three-way preferred, or 100 w. soft-white each. Check for 2 in./5 cm distance between top of bulb and top of shade to prevent the possibility of seeing the bulb when standing.

On a double dresser or particularly large dressing table it is better if the bottom diameter of the shades is 11 to 12 in. (28–30 cm) minimum and the bulbs are 50/100/150 w. three-way or 150 w. soft-white each.

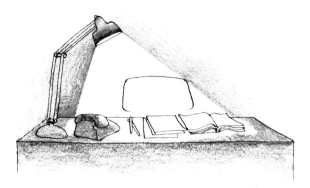

Desk and work tops

INCANDESCENT LAMPS should be 15 in./38 cm high to the lower edge of the shade, which is about eye level for the average adult.

The shade should be light, open at the top, and in a low-transmission material with a white or near-white lining.

The bulbs should be 200 w. or soft-white 50/200/250 w. three-way.

The center of the lamp shade should be 15 in./38 cm to left of work center (or to the right for a left-handed person) and 12 in./30 cm back from the front edge of the desk.

For swing-arm desk lamps, swing the shade closer to the front edge of the desk. For a drop-leaf desk a double swing-arm floor lamp is useful with the shade in the same position.

FLUORESCENT LIGHTED SHELVES are useful above deep desks or above workbenches or work tops. They save space and spread light over the entire desk width and can be custom made (see Chapter 6, "Do-It-Yourself Ideas," page 98) or purchased as a unit. The shielding board should be white inside, 4 to 5 in. (10–13 cm) and 15 to 18 in. (33–46 cm) above the desk top. The tube or tubes should be one or two 30 w. or 40 w. "warm white de luxe," or two GE Bright Stiks, and they should be mounted directly above the work center, 9 to 12 in. (23–30 cm) back from the front edge of the desk. If it is further back the reflection from the tube can be annoying. For essential upward light, leave a 2 in./5 cm strip open above the tube, which can be shielded with glass.

Light for sewing

FOR SEWING BY HAND, which usually means small needles and small stitches, you need twice as much light as for casual reading.

IF YOU USE A FLOOR LAMP, a double swing-arm is recommended, with a base height of 47 to 49 in. (119–124 cm), which is the average size, but if you can find a smaller one of 40 to 42 in. (102–107 cm), so much the better. The shade should be luminous or opaque with a 16 to 18 in. (41–46 cm) bottom, a 10 to 17 in. (25–43 cm) top, and a depth of 9 to 10 in. (23–25 cm). The bulbs should be 200 w., 50/200/250 or 100/200/300 w. three-way (at top level), or multiple sockets totaling 200 to 300 w.

IF YOU USE A TABLE LAMP, the bottom of the shade should measure 40 to 42 in. (102–107 cm) from the floor. The center of the shade should be 15 in./38 cm to the left of the work center (or to the right for left-handed persons) and 6 in./15 cm toward the rear of the chair. The same shade rules apply here as for floor lamps, except the depth could be 9 to 15 in. (23–28 cm), and it should take the same bulbs.

IF YOU HAVE BOUTS OF PROLONGED SEWING, working on fine detail, embroidery, or needlepoint, clamp an adjustable holder with a 75 w. R30 spotlight to the lamp shaft, or use a pole or tree lamp (a metal pole or rod with a weighted base and one, two, or three housings for spots) with adjustable bullet housing and a 75 w. R30 spotlight, or, alternatively, one of the small high-intensity portable lights positioned so that the shielded bulb is within 10 to 11 in. (25–28 cm) of the sewing.

FOR MACHINE SEWING you need more than just the combination of general lighting and the light provided by the tiny bulb on the machine.

IF YOU USE A FLOOR LAMP, choose a bullet-type pole or tree lamp with three light housings and black louvers for shielding. If there are no louvers the housing should be deep enough so that the end of the bulb is recessed at least 1 in./2.5 cm from the rim, with this 1 in./2.5 cm band painted matte black on the inside. It should be firmly adjustable so that you can aim the light absolutely accurately. Bulbs should

Far left top: Whenever possible, desk light should come from the side, as with this angled, adjustable desk lamp and wide beam. If there is no room for a lamp on the desk surface, light should come from above.

Far left bottom: A fluorescent strip is incorporated under the shelf above the desk in this sketch and gives even overall surface lighting. The strip could just as well be incandescent, of course.

Sewing sketch: The placing of this classic table lamp ensures adequate sewing light.

Top left: A double swing-arm reading lamp with a good-looking polished brass shade by Nessen.

Center left: A classic swing-arm lamp, also by Nessen.

Bottom left: A track fixture on a pin-up adaptor by Lightolier. This could be fitted into a great many useful places.

Above: Four types of lights that can be adjusted to throw light precisely on the task. The fixture by Morsa pinned up on the wall (far left) can be aimed up or down. The reflector-lamp holder (left), also by Morsa, can be clipped to a shelf and aimed in any direction. The housing by George Kovacs (right) has unlimited swiveling capacities; it can be used singly or in groups on a floor stand, as a table lamp, or as a pinup lamp. In the Morsa lamp at the far right, the universal swiveling function is present, but the construction of the flexible stand is the design feature.

be 75 w. R30 floods, or, as an alternative, a regular 75 w. or 100 w. bulb in the lower and middle units, with the same or up to 150 w. in the top unit if the fixture will take that much wattage.

Place the pole in line with the shoulder and 12 in./30 cm to the left (20 in./51 cm on a diagonal from the machine needle). Aim the lower light at the machine needle; aim the middle light at the work area and part of the wall behind the machine; and aim the top light at the ceiling and upper side wall for general surrounding light.

IF YOU USE A WALL LAMP, the shade should be open-topped with minimum dimensions of top 8 in./20 cm; depth 8 in./20 cm; bottom 13 in./33 cm.

The bulb should be 100 or 150 w., or 50/100/150 w. three-way and there need not be a diffuser. It should be mounted so that the lower edge of the shade is 14 in./36 cm above the table and the center is 12 in./30 cm to the left of the needle and 7 in./18 cm toward the rear.

IF YOU USE A CEILING FIXTURE, it is best to install an adjustable bullet reflector or a recessed "eyeball" fixture.

Use a PAR 38 150 w. flood or spot (the spotlight will put about twice the light in a smaller area), but remember that additional surrounding lighting will be needed for visual comfort.

Fix the chosen light on or in the ceiling, above a point 13 in./33 cm to the left of the needle, 7 in./18 cm toward the user, and tilted toward the needle location.

Light for reading piano music   The best methods for lighting a piano, or an organ placed against a wall, are recessed or surface-mounted adjustable fixtures, or track lighting located behind the user and aimed to cover music and the immediate background.

Bulbs should be 150 w. PAR floods.

Ideally, an adjustable ceiling-mounted "bullet" or recessed "eyeball" fixture should be located 24 in./61 cm out from the center of the music rack (over the player's head) and tilted to light the music and the wall at the rear of the piano.

Even better would be a pair of these "bullet" or "eyeball" fixtures located the same distance out and 20 in./51 cm to the left and right of the center of the music rack.

PORTABLE LAMP METHOD. If it is impossible to use ceiling-mounted fixtures as described, a double swing-arm floor lamp would be convenient. The shade should have an open top and a neutral color, and should give generous transmission of light. The minimum dimensions should be: top 10 in./25 cm; depth 10 in./25 cm; and bottom 16 in./41 cm.

The bulb should be 50/100/150 or 100/200/300 w. three-way, and it should be sited with the center of the shade or the socket 13 in./33 cm in front of the lower edge of the music rack and 22 in./56 cm to the right or left of keyboard center.

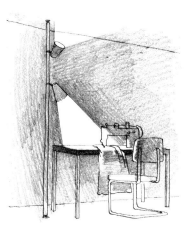

Above: This bullet-type tree lamp has the lower housing aimed at the needle part of the sewing machine, and the top housing aimed at the ceiling and upper wall for more general surrounding light

Right: A double track inset into the ceiling in this Manhattan room has one line for quartz bulbs and the other for low-voltage spots. The fixture above the piano is angled to light both music and keyboard. Interior design by Victoria and Ronald Borus; lighting by Ralph Bisdale.

Below: A double swing-arm floor lamp with an open-topped shade placed to the left of the keyboard center provides a feasible alternative to ceiling-mounted or recessed lighting for piano playing. The shade is wide enough to transmit light onto music and keyboard alike.

ACCENT OR DECORATIVE LIGHTING GROUP

For a wall of pictures, prints, wall hangings, or other art use recessed wallwashers as mentioned in Chapter 3, "General Planning," page 40, and in Chapter 7, "Lighting Art and Objects," page 119; or use surface-mounted strip like Plugmold, and mount it 24 in./61 cm from the wall for uniform coverage, with or without a baffle. Strips can be bought in any length with any number of sockets.

Or use track lighting with individual housings (or with bare bulbs) which are adjustable for spacing and aiming, making it possible to light individual pictures as well. The housings are for reflector bulbs of 25, 30, 50, 75, or 150 w.; for PAR 38 150 w. flood or spotlights; and for PAR 36 12-volt bulbs. But it is a good idea to get catalogs from either light-bulb or fixture manufacturers to find out the wattage and beam spread needed for your own specific picture sizes, and what distance away they should be from the light source for maximum results.

FOR INDIVIDUAL PAINTINGS AND OBJECTS use "pinhole" or "framing" projectors, recessed into the ceiling 36 to 42 in. (91–107 cm) from the wall, with their lenses and shutters adjusted so that the light thrown is exactly the size of the picture shape. This is really the ideal sort of light for this situation if it is at all possible to install them.

Or use individual surface-mounted fixtures similar to those specified for track lighting, or use them in conjunction with track.

In the case of a painting over a mantel, use uplighting from T10 25, 40, or 60 w., or R20 50 w. reflector bulbs concealed in a vase or housed in a small canister; or use one of the small high-intensity lamps aimed from below to avoid reflections in the picture glass.

If you use a conventional picture light mounted on the picture to light it from above, it should be as inconspicuous as possible, it should have a rotating reflector, and it should be adjustable from the wall to adapt to an extra-thick frame. The length of the reflector should be one-third to one-half the width of the picture. Use tubular 25 or 40 w. bulbs on 9 in./23 cm centers.

FOR PLANTS, FLOOR SCULPTURE, OR HANGINGS NEAR FLOOR LEVEL: Uplights concealed behind plants, in corners, or just by the object to be lit will either bounce light up or graze the given object with light. Or you can use a small adjustable floor spotlight.

Left: Track lighting with four angled spots evenly light up this painted wall by Stan Peskett as well as catching the quilted multitoned bedcovers in matching colors. This fantasy room is in a Washington, D.C., house designed by Larry Durham.

Above left: A track wallwasher by Lightolier. Note the auxiliary reflector in front of the bulb.

Above right: More spots from a track light the hanging baskets and plants in this sketch. Note how the light is angled slightly from the left.

ROOM
BY ROOM
GUIDE

Room by Room Guide

Once general lighting principles have been absorbed and the functions of the various fixtures are understood, it should be fairly easy to start the more precise area planning. But before going on to room-by-room suggestions, it is important to talk about the more generalized problems of safety, as well as what to do when a room—or any space—is really dark during the day.

THE SAFETY ANGLE

There are always certain potential-accident dark spots in a home:

- *Stairs if there are any (for falling down)*
- *Corridors, halls, and landing areas (for tripping up or slipping)*
- *Bathrooms and bedrooms late at night*

These areas can be especially dangerous if there are very young, very old, or very shortsighted members of a household. If you are not sure what parts of your home could be dangerous, walk around it at dusk (taking due care yourself, of course) with the house or apartment unlit. And even if your own eyes are perfectly sound and keen, remember that eyes generally deteriorate with age, so that the average 60-year-old needs twice as much light as the average 30-year-old, and that what seems tolerably safe to a healthy adult might not be so for the elderly—or for small children, who might also be afraid of the dark.

Stairs, corridors, landings, and hallways These should be well lit at all times with light directed on the floor to show changes in levels or surfaces (*you* might be familiar with the odd step down to another room, but your visitors won't be), and light directed to the walls to show switches and door handles. Stairs are safest when lit from the top of the flight so that the risers are in a fair amount of shadow but the treads and their projecting edges, or nosings, are accentuated. To avoid having too much shadow on the risers, and to show distinctly where the last stair ends, there should also be another light at the bottom of a flight.

In any event, stairs and corridors often have inadequate sources of natural light, especially in apartment houses, so they often need to be at least bolstered, if not entirely lit, by artificial light all the time. But whatever happens, never use an open-topped portable lamp in any place by a staircase where a person coming down can look directly into the light source and be momentarily blinded.

If you are starting a lighting plan from scratch, you could install miniature (say 4 w.) night lights in all the stair/landing areas—and in children's rooms—which could be left on all 24 hours of the day if wanted because they consume a minimum amount of electricity. Alternatively, you could have all lights controlled by dimmer switches so that they could be turned down to optimum low levels at night. An additional advantage to both these methods is that they deter burglars and prowlers.

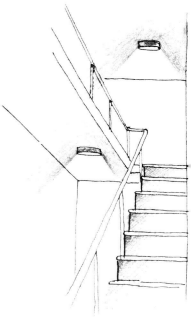

Preceding page, left: Adjustable spots pour light onto gleaming urns on polished steel bases at either side of the doorway. With the blue marbled walls and black-and-white floor, the effect is almost surrealistic. Lighting design by Ralph Bisdale in conjunction with interior designers Ronald and Victoria Corus.

Preceding page, right: A remarkable Lightolier fixture of clear glass bulbs put up by designer Bill Grover in a house in Connecticut. Photograph by Robert Perron.

Right: Two views of an Edwardian staircase in London lighted at the top of each flight for safety. In the top picture, a spot is also trained on the painting. A glass-doored closet in the picture below gives glow and interest to the area when properly lit. An uplight placed behind the table in the corner lights the pair of naïve prints just above.

Left: Always light the top and bottom of stairs as this sketch indicates.

Bedrooms and bathrooms   Bedroom lights that can be dimmed down for nighttime use or separate low-wattage night lights can be very comforting to children. Even luminous plugs which only consume 1 watt are some sort of comfort and will give out a steady glow.

Switching on lights at the normal level of intensity in a darkened room can cause temporary blindness and confusion—quite enough anyway for someone to trip over a light cord or a step—so much lower levels of illumination are needed in the small hours. Therefore, additional switches for low-wattage bulbs set right next to adults' beds could be especially useful for people who have to get up at night for whatever reason.

There are also far too many accidents caused by a disregard of common-sense safety rules: by the failure to replace old and faulty wiring; by loading too few outlets with too many appliances; by the careless use of appliances (and pull cords instead of switches near water—which can, of course, cause nasty if not fatal shocks), or by a thoughtless tangle of cords leading from wall outlets to floor and table lamps.

Coping with dark spaces   Obviously, extra windows are the best way of letting in more light during the day, but since extra or enlarged windows are not only expensive but often impossible to change or install, it is useful to list the cosmetic ways of achieving the same ends.

This does not mean just bumping up the wattage in all your light bulbs and painting all the ceilings and walls white. Different spaces and problems need a variety of different treatments, and there are several comparatively easy ways of adding to daylight rations in rooms that are starved of natural light.

LOW, DARK ROOMS are better with a white or very light ceiling and a light floor covering with—if possible—recessed ceiling lights or cornice lighting which will not take up any space. But if for one reason or another you would prefer to paint ceilings the same color as walls, avoid a lowering effect by painting any existing cornice or cove a brilliant white, or if no cornice exists, run a white strip around the walls underneath the ceiling.

ROOMS FACING NORTH AND EAST usually need warm colors rather than white or very light shades, which could be cold, so yellows, apricots, and pinks are best as light-givers here.

DO NOT USE DARK CURTAINS OR BLINDS. Light window coverings help reflect what daylight there is into a room. And make sure that curtain rods or rails are long enough to hang curtains on either side of the window frame so that no part of the glass is obscured.

ROLLER OR VENETIAN BLINDS OR SHUTTERS are obviously better light savers than curtains, since they can be rolled or folded neatly out of the way of any light. Or if a view is very dark and dreary and altogether better not seen, open louvered shutters with a concealed

Left: These two wall-mounted spots can be dimmed right down for low nighttime comfort and safety. Photograph by Robert Perron.

Right: Lighting designer Ralph Bisdale thought that the quartz bulbs in this suspended channel in a boy's room would provide a satisfyingly clear light for his work and other pursuits. Light thrown onto the ceiling and bounced back. Interior design by Ronald and Victoria Borus.

tungsten or fluorescent strip behind them will give the effect of letting in the sun while shutting out the dreariness.

LIGHT WALLS (see glossary and Chapter 6, "Do-It-Yourself Ideas") are also comparatively easy to install across windows with depressing views, as a backing for a series of shelves, or as a background for the display of art objects or curios. This sort of treatment will always pep up the given amount of daylight. Install strip lights on the old wall and conceal the fixtures about a foot behind sheets of translucent white or off-white plexiglass fitted into a wood frame or frames that can slide on runners attached to ceiling and floor, or remain static. Standard panels of plexiglass come in sizes of up to 4 by 8 ft. (122 by 244 cm), but they can be specially ordered in larger sizes.

CONCEALED VALANCE LIGHTING is always a good booster to daylight since it helps to frame windows as well as to reflect extra light onto a light-colored ceiling. Also, table or floor lamps placed on either side of a window in a dark space will increase the illusion of light coming in naturally.

STRIP LIGHTS CONCEALED BEHIND A FALSE CORNICE all around a room will subtly wash walls with light, and it is always useful to highlight a dark corner with a recessed eyeball spot in the ceiling or a concealed uplight on the floor.

BOOKSHELVES AND DISPLAY RECESSES LIT FROM WITHIN by concealed strip lights behind baffles or from concealed strips behind baffles just above the shelves, or with something like Lightolier's Lyte Trim, will also add to light and sparkle in a dark area.

A SUSPENDED LUMINOUS CEILING (with concealed light above) will give a much sunnier feel to a dark hall, kitchen, bathroom, or even living area, as long as it is supplemented at night in the latter case with good task and accent lighting. Otherwise it will be too bland.

In every room the main lighting aim should be to make each space as comfortable, easy to use, flexible, and safe as possible. You need to define vistas, identify focal points, and, most important, allow for the various functions of the room.

To help work out what is best where, first decide whether the space will be used more by day or by night; what type or types of lighting

Left: A fluorescent tube by Lightolier is attached under the wooden shelf holding plants and serves to light the wall as well as the plants massed underneath in this verdant area.

Right: Lightolier's Lyte Trim is fixed underneath these display shelves to give extra depth and interest to the objects, and indeed, to the shelves themselves.

should work most efficiently for your needs; whether any more electricity outlets, switches, or dimmers would be helpful; or indeed, whether the present wiring will stand up to any stretching of its capabilities. And think what style of fixture would *ideally* be best for each area. The ideals, unfortunately, will almost certainly have to be compromised once faced with any sort of budget restrictions, but at least you will have some sort of standard to aim for.

Here is a rundown of likely needs to cater to in each area.

HALLS, CORRIDORS, STAIRCASES

Since the hall is the first part of a home you see, it should at the very least be warm and welcoming. Yet all too often it is provided with only one ceiling outlet, which is usually quite inadequate.

The ideal is to have a series of downlights and wallwashers, either recessed, ceiling-mounted, or attached to track, set usually 3 ft./91 cm apart, which will provide reflected light off the walls, show off any wall decoration, and light up telephone, telephone books, mirror, and so on; or you can wash walls with small 50 w. R20 bulbs set on track about 1 ft./30 cm away from the wall and each other, concealed behind a baffle. Hall closets should certainly have an internal light, or else an angled light on the ceiling outside to avoid a constant irritating grope in the dark for coats.

That's the ideal. If it is not possible to recess lights, add extra surface-mounted fittings, or—as in a rental or for aesthetic reasons—add track to take the various fixtures from a single outlet, the only thing is to compromise. Run more cord from the original outlet and loop it across to another area, suspending the cord and an extra light from a ceiling hook. Alternatively, put uplights in corners,

Far left: Floor-to-ceiling fixed poles with adjustable housings mean that sculpture, window recesses, and ceiling can all be lighted with maximum flexibility.

Top left: Two ceiling-mounted spots and an uplight concealed behind the plant under the bottom shelf light up the recessed glass shelves in this Manhattan apartment designed by Mark Hampton.

Bottom left: Recessed downlights set about three feet apart give unobtrusive light to this long corridor. Photograph by Robert Perron.

Above: Ceiling-mounted downlights, bulbs concealed behind decorative octagonal Art Nouveau glass, and a concealed spot angled at the sculpture make a dramatic landing area in a Washington house designed by Larry Durham.

Left: A mixture of track lighting for background and accent light and extendable wall lamps above the sofa for comfortable reading give a relaxed light in this New York sitting room belonging to Tom and Noni Moore. A tall mirrored screen does triple duty in reflecting more light, adding to the seeming space, and disguising a storage and dumping area.

Below: A flexible "gooseneck" floor lamp allows light to be aimed in any direction. The lamp is by George Kovacs Lighting.

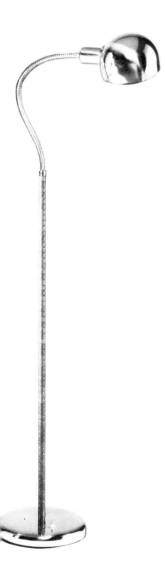

and, if there is at least a wall outlet, stand a lamp on a table, or a floor lamp on the floor. The "tree" or pole type of floor lamp with two or three swivel spots to be angled in various directions could be helpful as long as the spots are angled with care and do not shine straight into the eyes of someone walking in the front door.

As mentioned in the section on safety, if staircases are properly lighted there is a noticeable difference between tread and riser. The best way to achieve this is to have a strong light above the stairs and a softer one below. If the lights are on a dimmer switch they can be turned down to an acceptable level and left on all night with very little waste of energy. This is especially useful in households where there are old people or young children who might need to get up in the night. A more expensive alternative is to have a separate circuit of miniature low-wattage lights for nighttime use. A cheaper solution would be a single low-wattage fixture in a well-chosen position.

LIVING ROOMS

Sitting, relaxing, talking, entertaining, listening to music, playing music, reading, writing, sewing, and watching television are normal activities in most living rooms, with eating thrown in too, if there is a dining area (see the next section on dining rooms). The best light for all general living areas is, as noted in the chapter on general planning, a mixture of background, task, and accent lighting. (For background lighting see Chapter 3, "General Planning," pages 38–43.)

Lights for reading, sewing, writing, and playing the piano should be spaced and of the strength specified on pages 44–52.

Watching television in an otherwise dark room is a strain on the eyes. A light near the viewers will reflect in the screen, so a dimmed light like a spot or strip behind the set is best if the set is on a shelf. If the set is free-standing, use a dimmed downlight or a floor lamp shining at the wall.

Accent lighting can be provided in storage units and on shelves or in alcoves with the following methods. Collections of glass, ceramics, and small objects look their best in front of a translucent wall (made by fixing vertical strip lights to the wall behind the shelves and concealing them with panels of white plexiglass, acrylic, or glass. (See diagram in Chapter 6, "Do-It-Yourself Ideas," page 97; for the best lighting of art see Chapter 7, "Lighting Art and Objects.") Objects on shelves can also be picked out with tiny portable spots, and deeply recessed sections of wall units can be similarly treated.

Bookshelves can look especially dramatic when lit from the sides by strip lights concealed behind baffles, or from the top by lighting hidden behind a valance of some kind, or by wallwashers.

DINING ROOMS

The focal point of dining rooms and dining areas, whether in the living room or the kitchen, is the tabletop. One of the best ways to light it is to use downlighting from above, which should both light the

things on the table with the kind of "hard" light that makes china, glass, and silver sparkle and reflect light off the tabletop to light diners' faces from below. This angle is always the most flattering. (But if colored tablecloths are used they should be light tones of a warm color—pink for instance. Cool colors are less flattering: blue is too cold, green makes people look their worst.)

Any narrow-beam or medium-beam downlight can be used, and if the fixture is designed for use with a reflector bulb, you should use a PAR 38 flood bulb—150 w. if you are controlling the light with a dimmer, 75 w. if not (this assumes an average ceiling height of 8 to 9 ft. (2.5–2.7 m). If the fixture uses an ordinary A bulb, experiment with a clear 75 w. bulb rather than the inside-frosted variety because it should give more sparkle.

Downlighting can of course be produced by a variety of conventional and unconventional fixtures as well as actual downlights, but do be sure that the bulb is hidden from any normal (seated) viewing angle, and locate it high enough so that it will not prevent somebody on one side of the table from seeing somebody on the other, that is to say about 22 in./56 cm minimum above the tabletop.

All the downlight described so far produces a beam of light with a fairly soft edge, without sharp control, but a spectacular effect can be produced by using a framing projector shuttered so as to light the tabletop and nothing else (see Chapter 3, "General Planning," page 55). The contrast between the plane of the table, which is lit, and the other things and surfaces in the room, which are not directly lit, is very dramatic, making the tabletop appear to float.

If the room is already lit by a chandelier above the table, which is

Left: Downlight shines through the elaborate chandelier and onto the chrome and black Lucite table in a colorful dining room designed by the Boruses. Uplights are placed inside the window recess to graze the curtain fabrics with extra light. Even the floor picks up the shine.

Right: Candlelight is invariably flattering to room and diners alike, but the flame must be above or below eye-level so as not to cause glare. If possible, combine candles with some suitably dimmed background light. In Dr. Shirley Wray's dining room in Cambridge, Massachusetts, candles are backed by uplights in front of the blind and a strip behind the cornice that runs around the paneling.

eceding pages: When lighting
signer Ralph Bisdale was asked to
laborate with Ronald and Victoria
rus on the apartment shown on this
e, they decided that it was important
light the room through the art and
t the art must be lit in the most
autiful way possible. To this end,
dale designed a double recessed
tangular track to fit in subtly with
crown molding. One line of track
ds quartz bulbs, which give an
n, satisfying light to the larger
ntings; a second, low-voltage track
ts smaller paintings and objects.
e quartz lights are also used
r plants and unobtrusively perform
same function as grow lights. In
lition, one or two recessed lights are
ced in the center of each room to
vide walk-through light when neces-
y. Another bonus of this lighting plan
hat it completely obviates any
he low hum that is all too often
ard.

ft: In this dining room in Brooklyn,
ls are covered in blue glass and
ts are judiciously placed to light the
nches in the large urns as well as
urns themselves. A pair of candela-
make glass and cutlery sparkle. De-
n by Barbara Littman.

normally more handsome than the light it throws, the quality of light could be much improved by adding light from some other fixtures, especially recessed downlights (which will not compete with the chandelier for attention), and especially if the chandelier is made of crystal, which will then be caught in the beam of the downlights and made to sparkle (or gleam, if brass).

If, for reasons of economy, your landlord's regulations, or just taste, you cannot or do not want to use downlights, or if you do not possess a chandelier to boost with downlights anyway, you can always use candles alone on the table. They should be either above or below eye level, and combined with suitably dimmed background light in other parts of the room. Otherwise the contrast between flickering flames and surrounding darkness, though dramatic, is uncomfortable for the eyes.

Any serving area should of course be lit separately, perhaps by a dimmable spot, a wallwasher, or strip lighting concealed by a valance or cornice. Gentle background lighting can also be provided by uplights.

KITCHENS

A kitchen should have good general light plus localized light over the work tops for any precise activity like assembling ingredients, chopping, mixing, studying cookbooks, or washing dishes. Too many rooms have a ceiling light and nothing else, when the ideal would be to have well-placed general diffusing lights (see glossary) fixed flush to the ceiling, or inset spots and downlights plus strip lights concealed under high-level cupboards to shine at the right angle on the work surface and stove. Any fluorescent lights should be of the "warm white de luxe" variety, or mixed to produce a warm light of this sort.

Left: A rectangle of track in this kitchen designed by William Murphy and Louis Muller holds adjustable spots to light work tops and give general light to the pleasantly long room.

Right: A good-looking pendant fixture which gives a pleasantly diffused light. From Habitat, Inc., New York.

Top left: Two downlights set above a curved saucepan rack give extra shine and interest to the equipment as well as lighting the work surface underneath. Uplight shows up the rainbow-and-cloud-painted side wall. Photograph by Robert Perron.

Bottom left: Detail of the glass canopy shown in the big picture at right. The light thrown through the glass is pleasantly diffused. Design by Ronald and Victoria Borus in conjunction with lighting designer Ralph Bisdale.

Above: A high-hat downlight grazes the texture of the stripped brick in this kitchen as well as lighting the open wood shelves. Another downlight gives more general light to the room and to the refectory table underneath. Photograph by Robert Perron.

Right: Spots mounted on the extractor outlet sparkle through the glass canopy and more light is diffused through the glass panels in the storeroom doors in this kitchen designed by Borus and Borus in conjunction with Ralph Bisdale.

Storage cupboards should be lit from the inside as well with some sort of strip lighting, and if there is a dining area it should be treated as described in the dining-room section, with other light either switched off or preferably dimmed.

BEDROOMS
Bedroom lighting needs to be as flexible as that in the living area, with the same mixture of general, task, and accent light for dressing, making up, and reading in bed. The right sort and placement of lamps for reading in bed and for dressing tables is described in Chapter 3, "General Planning," pages 45–47. Remember, a small light above a mirror used for making up is not good because it casts shadows under the nose and eyes. Lights that are side-positioned to shine outward, rather than on the mirror itself, are better. The same applies to long mirrors; the light should be directed on the viewer rather than on the glass.

CHILDREN'S ROOMS
All outlets should be childproofed, at least in the rooms of small children, and lighting fixtures and cords should be kept well out of reach. Dimmer switches are especially useful for children who are afraid of the dark, or for infants, because the light can be turned down to a gentle glow. Alternatives are a single low-wattage bulb, a separate—but expensive—circuit of low-wattage lights, or luminous plugs.

Do not forget that older children will want to read in bed and probably do homework, drawing, painting, model making, and so on in their rooms, so provide adequate reading lights in the right positions, as well as desk-top or work-top light.

BATHROOMS AND POWDER ROOMS
If a bathroom directly adjoins a bedroom, the change in light between the two rooms should not be too abrupt. The main light source in a bathroom is usually provided by a light over the mirror if the room is very small, boosted by a central ceiling fixture with reflected light from white or neutral surfaces below, and perhaps by illuminated shelves. If the room is larger, downlight above bath and basins, boosted by a shaving/makeup light around the mirrors, is better. Showers or closed-in tubs need a recessed vapor-proof fixture with the switch outside the shower area.

Small powder rooms are usually adequately lit by light at top and sides of the mirror, which will not cause shadows to fall on the face.

Top right: Strips of white bulbs in a Lightolier fixture are installed on the mirror above this bath as well as onto a wall for general lighting. Since both sets of light are reflected in the mirror, the light is effectively doubled.

Bottom right: Clear glass balls of light stud this mirrored bathroom like oversize pearls and are reflected in the mirrored ceiling in a true "Play of Brilliants" (see page 31). Both photographs by Robert Perron.

Far left: Counter a dark workroom with large fluorescent fixtures (remembering that laundries should have 100 maximum).

Left: Concentrate light on an intricate hobby task from both sides.

Right: In this billiard room in Washington, D.C., designed by Larry Durham with murals by Stan Peskett, an incandescent industrial reflector is hung over each half of the table. A mixture of downlights and wallwashers along the perimeter of the room provide background light as well as setting off the painted walls.

Below: A fluorescent industrial fixture throws light upon a pool table.

UTILITY AND LAUNDRY ROOMS

General lighting is needed here, with specific lighting for jobs like ironing. For recommended light level see the table in Chapter 3, "General Planning," page 43. Working surfaces can be lit in the same way as kitchen counter tops with fluorescent strips mounted behind baffles to cast light down. Ironing is best when a shadow-eliminating light is used above and in front of the ironer.

If you are lighting a fixed ironing board, the ideal would be fixtures for 75 w. reflector floodlights mounted on or in the ceiling 48 in./122 cm apart and 24 in./61 cm ahead of the front edge of the board and aimed at its surface. When ironing with a portable ironing board anywhere else in the home, place a floor lamp close to the center of the board opposite the ironer. It should house a minimum of 150 w. Alternatively, the pole lamp with three louvered bullets also works well because the middle and lower lights can direct sharp light on to the board at a wrinkle-revealing angle, and the top light could be directed upward.

GAME ROOMS
(AND GENERAL LIGHTING FOR HOBBIES)

PERMANENT CARD TABLES could have four 75 w. reflector floodlights in recessed or surface-mounted fixtures placed 2 ft./61 cm out diagonally from each corner of the table so that cards are well lit in players' hands.

PING-PONG TABLES could have fixtures centered over the ends of the table using, for example, two surface-mounted, well-shielded 30 or 40 w. fluorescent fixtures, or one 150 w. silvered-bowl bulb with a metal reflector. If the ceiling is very low, say only 6½ to 7 ft. (2–2.1 m), use two recessed 30 or 40 w. fluorescent bulbs above the center and ends of the table; or one recessed incandescent box, 13 in./33 cm square for a 150 w. bulb over each corner of the table.

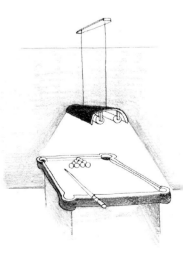

POOL TABLES. Center one recessed 150 w. reflector floodlight over each half of the table; or suspend two 40 w. fluorescent fixtures (again, centered over each half of the table) so that the bottom of each fixture is 36 in./91 cm above the table.

DECORATING
WITH LIGHT
& LIGHTS

Decorating with
Light and Lights
Up to now we have discussed general home lighting and its possibilities without going very much into the use of light as an integral part of the architecture and furnishing of a room.

We are told that room size and feel can be visually controlled by the lighting, and we know that this is achieved by the amount of light we use, and how and where we place it. But we must always keep in mind that light itself is invisible—when you see, you are not seeing light, but the reflections from lighted surfaces. In other words, a surface is "dark" because it *absorbs* light, and it is "light" because it *reflects* light. Dark room surfaces, particularly walls, seem to drop away and lose importance so that the objects and people in the space tend to become more important, and the space less so. This is dramatic but sometimes leads to a certain tenseness. In very light and all-white rooms people can, on the contrary, feel quite insignificant and disoriented.

So unless you have a particular reason for making a very dark or a very light room, you should try to make room surfaces reflect light in such a way that relative brightnesses correspond to sky, landscape, and earth with the ceiling brightest, the walls less so, and the floor least of all. Because it is natural, we are easy with this sort of balance.

In practice, it is comfortable to aim for a 70 percent or higher reflectance for ceilings, 50 percent or higher for walls, and 15 percent or higher for floors. A very rough list of reflectances from familiar surfaces would run as follows:

- *Matte black paint—less than 5 percent*
- *Dark floors and woodwork, say charcoal grey, dark green, or medium blue—10 to 15 percent*
- *Denim blue, cherry red, medium greens—15 to 30 percent*
- *Light oak, pine, ordinary sand, light-colored stone—30 to 50 percent*
- *Aluminum paint, off-white, light peach, apricot pink, and light yellow—50 to 75 percent*
- *White paint, good commercial ceiling-tile materials, plaster, and snow—over 75 percent*

One superb example of a space almost entirely decorated with light is Clive Summers' hairdressing salon in the Olympic Tower in New York City. It is a large room with no windows at all, yet it looks as glowing and light and airy as if perpetually flooded with sunlight. The whole effect has been achieved by painting the walls and ceiling a warm peach and concealing light fixtures in the ceiling under a large shirred panel of peachy gauze draped over simple rods.

If you want to emphasize a particular room, as opposed to the people and objects within it, you can exaggerate and expand its apparent size by projecting extra brightness on the walls. This is best done as explained earlier, by wallwashers either recessed into the

Preceding page, left: A wall of mirror and hanging lights in Paul Rudolph's apartment.

Preceding page, right: Lightolier's Banner Lytetiles form amazing ceilings. They consist of natural linen squares like medieval banners to frame and square off Lytetile mirrors inset with their bare-bulb fixtures. There are two choices: matte white tiles, white bulbs, and oatmeal-colored banners for a warm natural light; mirror chrome tiles white linen banners, and clear bulbs to make a room seem misty and ethereal. All the banners are weighted to keep their shape.

Right: Every surface in this kitchen (by Ronald and Victoria Borus in conjunction with lighting designer Ralph Bisdale) reflects light in the natural order: ceiling brightest, with the skylight and large Italian diffusing fixture; walls next, with strings of small Italian spots linked around the edges of the room; tiled floor, which merely reflects. The effect is very comfortable.

ceiling, surface-mounted, or mounted on track. These last never manage to light the wall as evenly as the more sophisticated stationary equipment (they do not throw the light as far down the wall or spread it as widely, resulting in "hot spots," or areas of uneven brightness). Very careful aiming of the fixtures, however, can usually overcome the worst of these problems, and it is certainly much easier to mount lights on track than to recess or ceiling-mount them.

In fact, the easiest way to light a whole wall is to install a number of simple lamp holders on track, about 1 ft./30 cm apart, and about the same distance from the wall, and to aim them vertically downward. (Do not tilt them toward the wall; try to reach the bottom of the area and the top will take care of itself.) For an average 8 to 9 ft. (2.4–2.7m) ceiling height, use General Electric 50 w. R20 bulbs. This row of bulbs can either be left exposed or concealed behind a valance of some sort. Lightolier makes a prefabricated valance just for this purpose, with a notch for the attachment of track.

Light can also be used in the most diverse ways to enhance and decorate walls as well as to accent them. Luminous walls or wall panels can be made fairly painlessly (see Chapter 6, "Do-It-Yourself Ideas"). Moving patterns and images can be projected onto vertical surfaces by lighting projectors or spotlights shining through rotating wheels of colored lenses. Spots can be shone through any chosen object to cast shadows, and colored filters can be fitted over bulbs to totally change the mood and feeling of a room. And the lighting decoration doesn't have to be confined to walls. Tables or seating platforms, sofas, and unit seating can be defined with ribbons and rims of light which make the furniture appear to float off the floor, or away from the walls. Many of these treatments are explained and illustrated in the next chapter.

You can also decorate with points of light—another way of making light work for you. Candles are probably the most familiar, the most interesting, and certainly the most flattering way of decorating with separate accent lights; they can be used in imaginative ways to provide the "Play of Brilliants" Richard Kelly was talking about (quoted in Chapter 3). But unless a room is filled with them—with suitable guards against fire risk—they should not be used on their own without some sort of gentle background light because the intense flickering flames are too much contrast against general darkness.

Neon lamps are also much used as decoration. Aside from amusing old neon signs there are fanciful standing shapes like hearts, lips, cacti, ice cream cones, or what you will in many different colors; and shapes that can be mounted on the wall or used on ceilings. Their drawbacks are their fragility, the buzzing noise that comes as part of the package, and the rather heavy transformers that need to be used.

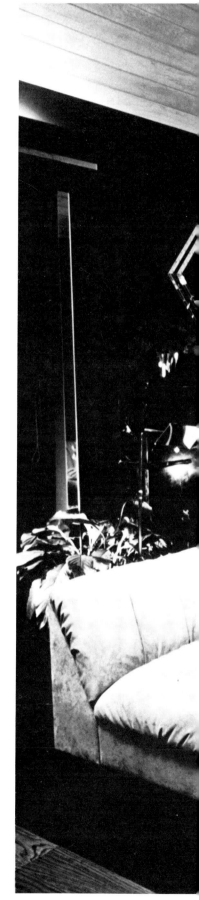

Oil lamps, too, provide an especially mellow light, and nostalgia must give a great spur to design because there is a galaxy of both candle holders and good-looking new oil-lamp designs around. After candles the most usual decorative lighting is with tiny bulbs like the Christmas-tree variety, which can actually look festive all year round draped in trees, clustered as centerpieces, and used in a dozen different ways. The most practical of these little bulbs are the kind that are held by being pushed and turned into a socket (high-intensity bulbs usually fit this way as well). Bigger bulbs can be very ornamental too. Some years ago, the Tovi lamp company introduced a round bulb that had a very thin coating of aluminum. When this is not turned on it looks like a perfect silver sphere. When it is lit it becomes a most interesting-looking light, with multiple reflections of the filament glittering inside the glass ball. It is now made and sold by the major companies and should be widely available.

Incandescent lamps of course come in all shapes and sizes, especially those from Italy and France, and can be used rather like sculpture. And certainly some of the early modern Italian designs are now as much twentieth-century classics as the Mies Barcelona chair, or the Corbusier chaise-longue.

Preceding page: A room designed by Richard Knapple of Bloomingdale's seems to be rimmed with light. In fact, the dark walls and curved ceiling set off the arched strips of steel surrounding the door and the vertical strips delineating the long windows, which catch and refract light from uplights as well as tubular lights concealed above the window valances, themselves trimmed with steel. Incidentally, the same sort of effect could be achieved with the offcut and trimmings from mirror factories.

Above: In this dining room, candlelight on the mantelpiece as well as on the table provides most of the light, but it is backed by gentle light behind the urn pedestals, which picks out the curtain border as well as adding a gleam to the urns in the window embrasures.

Right: Tubes fitted with Christmas-tree-like bulbs make a decorative light sculpture in this dining area, as well as adding some extra background light to the candles. Photograph by Robert Perron.

DO IT YOURSELF IDEAS

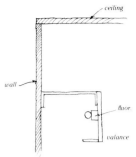

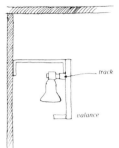

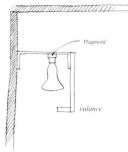

Do It Yourself Ideas

Anyone who is handy can obviously save a lot of money and frustration by adding to or improving his or her own lighting. Most materials are easily available from electrical distributors, hardware stores, or local building supply houses. We are *not* suggesting rewiring on your own (except for small things like adding a new outlet or a dimmer switch) because this is complicated and is much more safely done by a professional—or at the very least by someone who has proved to be competent in this field. But we *are* giving suggestions and ideas for overcoming the most common problems, as well as showing how to accentuate various furnishings.

Once again, we have listed suggestions under the various room headings because this seems logical and easy to follow. But before you plunge enthusiastically into building half a dozen luminous shelves or so, do check on the structure of your home, especially the walls and ceilings. Apartment dwellers in particular should check with the superintendent of their building before starting any drilling; this will protect both parties against lease regulations, and he should be able to tell you what type of construction material is used in your building and how best to anchor in screws. Also:

- *Be sure that all fixtures and fixture parts are U.L. listed, or given the standard listing of the country concerned.*
- *Rather than using extension cords, which may become hazardous, especially if the plug is not pushed tightly into the outlet, replace cords with new ones that are long enough for the purpose. In the U.S., the National Electrical Code is quite explicit about flexible cords and their uses. To quote: "Flexible cords and cables shall not be used (1) as a substitute for the fixed wiring of a structure; (2) where run through holes in walls, ceilings, or floors; (3) where run through doorways, windows, or similar openings; (4) where attached to building surfaces; or (5) where concealed behind building walls, ceilings, or floors."*

- *Beware of stress on wires by pulling them too tightly and twisting where tight stress may create wiring hazards.*

- *Use grounding cord if near water.*

- *Be sure no electric wiring is supporting a fixture unless you use a fitting made for the purpose. (in other words do not hang fixtures from electric wire; use chain or some other material).*

- *To conceal wiring, run it along corners or molding and paint to match.*

- *When changing switches to dimmers, be sure all electrical current is turned off; the same applies for adding a new outlet and for any wiring and electrical work.*

Every locality is governed by some kind of electrical code. For an authoritative interpretation of the requirements affecting you, it is essential that you consult the local governing body. This can be done directly or through an architect, a consulting engineer, a licensed electrical contractor, or even perhaps a knowledgeable vendor, but it is up to you to find out the specific rules governing your application. What we have listed is only a general summary of the most important facts.

Preceding page, left: In Yann Weymouth's New York loft, cut-out squares and circles in the partition wall allow views into kitchen, bathroom, and utility areas, but the most interesting visual effects of all are the different moods evoked by the switching of different-colored fluorescent tubes concealed in a trough above the wall.

Preceding page, right: A Morsa floor lamp to give a pleasant, soft general light. It is available from Abitare, 212 E. 57th Street, New York City, or Morsa, 182 Hester Street, NYC. For other sources, write to Morsa at their New York City address.

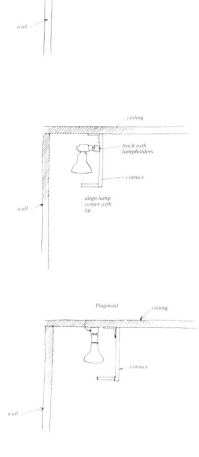

Above left: Sketches showing how to install fluorescent strips (top), track lights (center), or Plugmold strips (bottom) behind a valance.

Above right: These sketches show how fluorescent strips (top), track lights (center), or Plugmold strips (bottom) are installed behind a cornice.

Right: Cheap gooseneck factory lights were fitted with colored bulbs—each one different and worked from a dimmer switch—and screwed into a wooden ceiling plate by British designer William Waldron in an early hi-tech effect. The cost was minimal for maximum lighting.

IDEAS FOR GENERAL LIVING AREAS

Make your own canister lights   You can visually expand small rooms by lighting vertical surfaces, but surface-mounted canister-type lights can be expensive. Try making them instead out of juice cans, using 50 w. reflector lamps. Hang them from hooks in the ceiling and place the centers of the fixtures 6 to 8 in. (15–20 cm) from the surface to be lighted. This will graze the walls with light and accent the texture if any.

Homemade cornices, brackets, and valances   You can also light walls with homemade cornices and brackets, cutting the shielding board to match the style of the room. And you can light curtains with a valance.

Putting up track   It is not difficult to put up surface-mounted electrified track, either. The advantage of this is that it can be disconnected and moved whenever you do, and that any fixtures put on it are removable and adjustable so you can use spots for highlight-

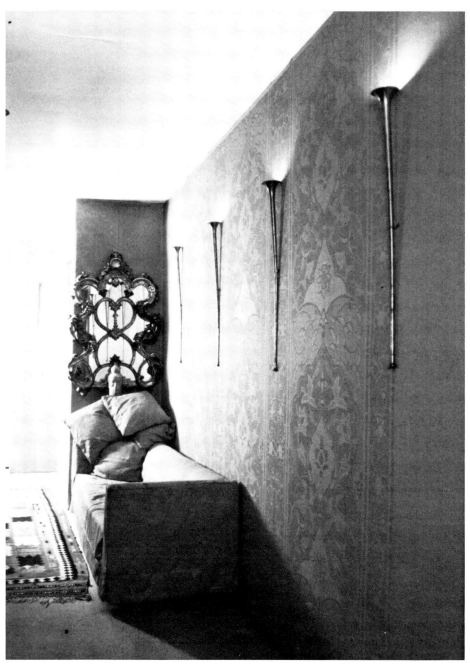

ing, or downlights to graze the surface, or wallwashers to flood the wall with light. And with various multicolored bulbs and filters you can also play around with color as much as you like. But the average 15 amp circuit in a normal room can supply up to about 1,200 watts of power, so do be sure to add up the wattage of each bulb on the track and add the result to any other lights in the room so that you don't exceed the limit and blow a fuse. (Actually, a 15 amp fuse can theoretically take a load of up to 1,800 watts, but getting anywhere near that is asking for trouble.)

Left: In fabric designer Michael Szell's London hall, he has inset bulbs into a collection of horns to make interesting do-it-yourself lighting.

Top right: You can make your own canister lamp out of an old juice can using a 50 w. reflector bulb, and piercing a hole big enough to hold the screw or bayonet fitting and the wire.

Bottom left: Two 25 w. R 14 bulbs or their equivalents can be positioned in opposite corners beneath an end table with a bottom shelf and pointed down to light an object resting on the shelf. They could be fitted on mini-track like Lightolier Lyte Trim, which fits in neatly.

Bottom center: Alternatively, you could fit in a grow-light tube to both light and help plants' growth. Or use a General Electric Lightstik.

Bottom right: A bare bulb or a small uplight underneath a white acrylic table will produce a luminous cube.

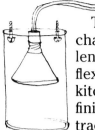

There are two kinds of track to choose from. Continuous open-channel track is very flexible. Fixtures twist in anywhere along its length and can be easily swapped around. Closed channels are not so flexible, but they are neat, protected from grease and steam (good for kitchens), and can be painted along their bottom edge for a cleaner finish. In this case, fixtures plug into outlets along the length of the track.

Both types of track are sold in various lengths and finishes, often prewired and polarized to assure a properly grounded electrical connection. They snap together easily, and with flexible corner connectors they can be used at any angle. Mount the track on the ceiling, up the wall, or along the top of the baseboard by knocking out the pre-stamped circles in the top of the track and inserting appropriate wooden screws or toggle bolts through the holes. But if the building is made from concrete, drill holes with a carbide-tipped bit, insert a lead or plastic anchor, and use a sheet-metal screw, $\frac{1}{2}$ in./1 cm longer than the plug, to secure the track to the surface.

Lighting furniture   Furniture can be lighted very easily as well, giving it quite an unexpected fillip.

END TABLES with lower shelves can be lit with two 25 w. R14 reflector lamps positioned in opposite corners and pointing down. This will give highlights and shadows to objects on the shelves as well as subtle accent lighting.

LIGHT BEHIND SOFAS AND OTHER LARGE PIECES. Fluorescent fixtures can be used behind sofas, buffets, credenzas and so on. This will give a wash of light up the wall behind, as well as accenting any objects or art on the walls. Fluorescent lighting, of course, has the advantage of not getting hot, so it will not scorch your furniture. Or simply move furniture out from the wall a little and place small uplights on the floor behind.

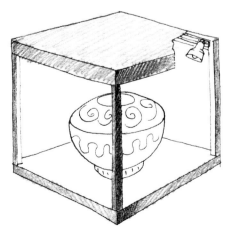

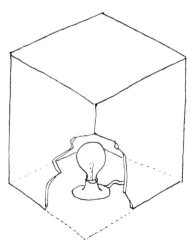

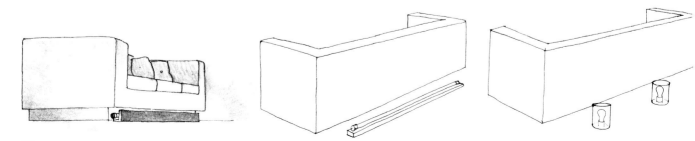

Left: A small pair of lamps on the dressing table in this bedroom have shades with cut-out backs that can be swiveled around to cast extra light on the face. Fabric-hung walls are lit here and there by uplights on the floor, and occasional sparkle is provided by the candles on the mantelpiece below the mirror. Note fabric looped back at either side of the chest of drawers, as at the windows. Design by Mary Gilliatt.

Right: This glass-fronted armoire is lit from within by incandescent tubes concealed behind the door, and from outside by a row of giant-size clear glass bare bulbs. Photograph by Robert Perron.

Below left: Float a sofa or seating units on a ribbon of light by installing strips of Plugmold on the base, covered with translucent material.

Below center: Wash the wall behind a sofa with a fluorescent strip or alternatively with incandescent uplights.

Below right: Sketches show the positioning of light strips installed in a glass-fronted cupboard as in the photograph of the armoire above.

ARMOIRES, GLASS-FRONTED BOOKCASES, SECRETARIES, AND WELSH DRESSERS can be lighted with tubular incandescent or fluorescent bulbs mounted inside the door heading or on the inside of the door, which will allow light to spill through the door if these are louvered or have shaped or grilled fronts. In the case of a Welsh dresser or open-shelved secretary, tubular lights can be fixed up the sides of the shelves just behind the framework, which is usually quite deep. Wiring can be pulled through a small hole drilled in the back.

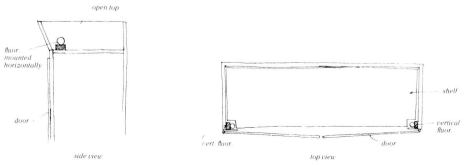

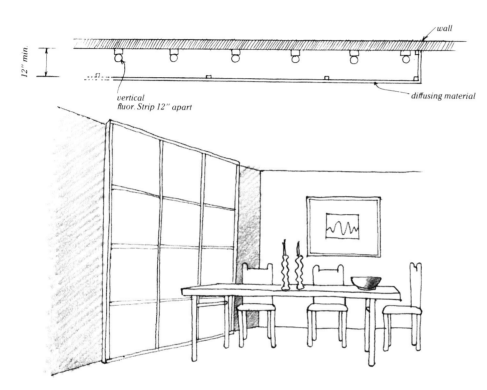

vertical
fluor. Strip 12" apart

12" min.

wall

diffusing material

Left: Cutaway top view showing construction of luminous wall panel in the sketch below. Fluorescent bulbs or strips of small incandescent bulbs are fastened to the wall, and translucent material stretched on a frame is then fixed over the whole so that the light glows through.

Right: A translucent screen framed in wood makes an effective backing for the dining table here, and is especially well placed at right angles to the window with its Venetian blinds, which forms its own different kind of luminous panel. Note that it is essential to use a dimmer with these luminous panels and screens to avoid annoying brightness.

Luminous panels and translucent screens These can be used for vertical surface lighting, as room dividers, and for lighting dark halls and corners. They are not particularly difficult to make from scratch (see illustration above).

Shelving units and cabinets Shelves can be lit in such a way as to add interesting accents as well as to provide functional light for the area. Luminous shelves are one possibility. These can be made from diffusing plastic or frosted glass covering a fluorescent bulb and framed with wood, and can be used either as the shelves themselves or as backing. Cabinets can also be illuminated on the inside or outer top (the light at the top will also illuminate the cabinet front when the door is closed) with either incandescent or fluorescent light. And a mixture of the two—while not the easiest thing to accomplish—can create an interesting effect. Strip lights can be concealed up the insides and shielded with a baffle, or run across the top and concealed by a valance.

Ribbons of light These are successful when made with strips of Plugmold run around the bases of sofas and chairs to make them appear to float. The strips are then covered with a translucent material tucked into a slim frame.

Left: Work in your own shadow (left) because you have a wrongly placed light fixture, or place the fixture over the task (right), i.e., under the cabinets, and work in a comfortable light.

Right: A fluorescent tube is concealed under the hood over the range and working top, and fluorescent tubes are mounted on the underside of the cupboards above the sink and extra work top in Dr. Shirley Wray's kitchen. The glazed splashback reflects more light back into the room.

Below: Place a downlight over the sink, if there is room, for effective task light.

IDEAS FOR KITCHENS AND EATING AREAS

Kitchen working surfaces   The best way to light counter tops is to mount fluorescent channels to the undersides of cabinets, as close to the front as possible. You can either side-mount the channels and use the back of the channel as a shield, or cut shielding from quarter-inch plywood to fit in with the style of the kitchen.

You can use this same arrangement over the sink and stove areas if you have convenient undersides of cabinets above. Alternatively, mount a bullet-type fixture on the side of the nearest cabinet and aim it at the task area. Wiring can be run through a small hole drilled in the cabinet. Again, a luminous shelf as described for living-room shelving units can be effective.

Pantry or closet doors can also become unexpected light sources. Use a door with a translucent or glass panel, one that is half-glazed, or one that has a decorated panel inset like stained glass. Put a light in the closet if there is not one already, and leave it on. It often adds an unexpectedly interesting accent to a room. You can also use incandescent strips, which are cheaper to buy but more expensive to run—though better to work under as well as lighting the food more attractively.

Because the lights in the kitchen are often left burning many hours in a day, it might be wise to consider using a large fluorescent fixture —2 ft. × 4 ft. (610 cm × 1220 cm) or 30 in. by 30 in. (760 cm × 760 cm)—for a large area of light. The fixtures can be recessed, but are easier to install surface-mounted. As we said previously, fluorescent can be dimmer-controlled as well.

Track lighting for more general light   Closed-channel tracks, described on page 95, could be useful here, fixed in exactly the same way. Fixtures can be aimed at cabinets, up on the ceiling, and used as downlight as well.

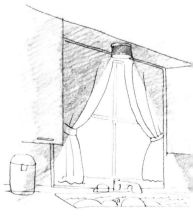

Left: In Paul Rudolph's apartment, ribbons of light underneath the seating platforms are formed from concealed Plugmold strips, which make the seating appear to float insubstantially above the floor. The floor in turn is traced with rows of tiny inset bulbs, more or less invisible by day but with extraordinary effect by night. The transparent strips of vinyl that form a dividing screen behind the table catch and refract this sparkling "Play of Brilliants" (see page 31).

Right: Architects Louis Muller and
William Murphy designed this sitting
room in a beach co-op on Fire Island.
A wooden trough running the length of
the apartment is filled with incandescent
tubes that light the sloping, beamed
ceiling. A strip of Plugmold clipped
with regularly spaced bare bulbs is concealed behind the seating platform to
light the long expanse of bare white
wall. A rangy adjustable lamp provides
reading and accent light whenever it is
needed.

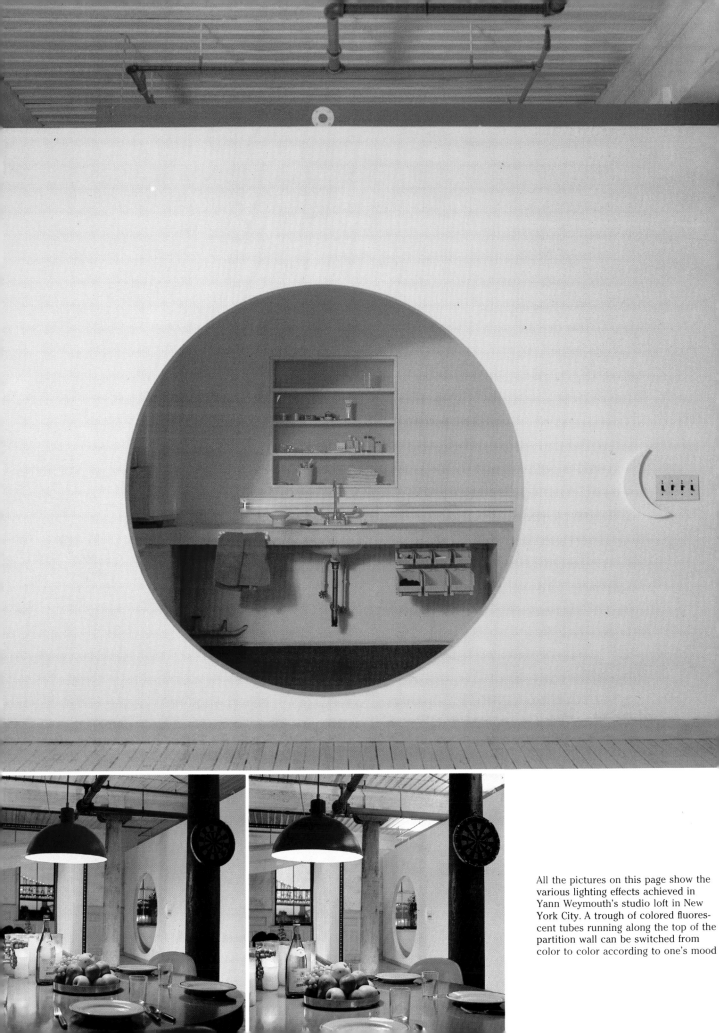

All the pictures on this page show the various lighting effects achieved in Yann Weymouth's studio loft in New York City. A trough of colored fluorescent tubes running along the top of the partition wall can be switched from color to color according to one's mood

Page 104: In this apartment designed by architects William Muller and Louis Murphy, an uplight is placed immediately under the glass top of the curved table and reflects off the curved white dish suspended above. Plugmold is recessed into the stepped level of the floor to make a kind of lighted broadwalk of the carpet. Two Luxor lights illuminate the sides of the room, and more light is reflected from the pivoting mirrored door.

Page 105: Teen-ager Sophia Gilliatt worked out all lighting in this room herself, as well as installing a sound/light system to work with the music center in conjunction with a friend, Andrew Dawood. Note the collection of decorative lights: the ice-cream-cone neon, and the painted cotton cover with a pink bulb inside.

Page 106: A supergraphic hall is lit by colored bulbs fixed onto walls at the side. It leads to the children's quarters and is a suitable preview of the playroom to come.

Page 107: The lighting in this supergraphic bathroom is exactly what we have said not to do for adults in other parts of the book, but the room is still fun for kids who don't yet need to shave or apply makeup.

Left: Accent lights are fixed to old pipes and joists here, which support a length of track very felicitously. Photograph by Robert Perron.

Below: A luminous shelf to light up and down (see page 98 under Shelving Units and Cabinets for the idea).

Right: A curving line of architectural strips march down the ceiling of this room like railroad cross ties. They combine with the recessed and baffled spots on the left to form an interesting lighting scheme. Design by Dexter Design.

Dining rooms and areas There are more possibilities for lighting in dining rooms than any other room in the house. For some occasions, candles alone—if there are enough of them—would be fine; for other occasions, several picture lights alone work quite well.

And a centerpiece made of tangles of Chistmas-tree lights with an arrangement, say, of foliage, gives plenty of light for a festive occasion.

Downlight is the best light over a table, as we have already discussed in Chapter 4, "Room-by-Room Guide," but for additional interest it is not hard to build a luminous buffet or serving shelf. This can be mounted on right-angle brackets and is built on the same principle as the luminous shelves but made deeper.

To control the lighting level in the room and to give flexibility to mood and atmosphere, place any lights in the room on dimmers. These can easily be wired into the wall-switch outlet.

BATH AND DRESSING AREAS

MIRROR LIGHTING. Bathroom lighting is so often inadequate. If there is just one incandescent fixture over the mirror it *can* be improved by replacing the old fixture with a new one containing two or three bulbs. Although this is better, it will still fail to do its job properly in that it will fail to light the side of the face.

One way to solve this problem is to use "plug-in" strips on either

Left: Strips of small white bulbs edge the mirrored surround and backing of this basin, and reflect onto the shiny ceiling as well as providing excellent makeup and shaving light.

Top right: Light from behind a mirror creates a soft glow that is decorative as well as practical.

Bottom right: Plugmold with receptacles to make a strip of indandescent light. Any sort of lights can be plugged in.

Below: This is the ideal light for making up and is consistently used in theatrical dressing rooms.

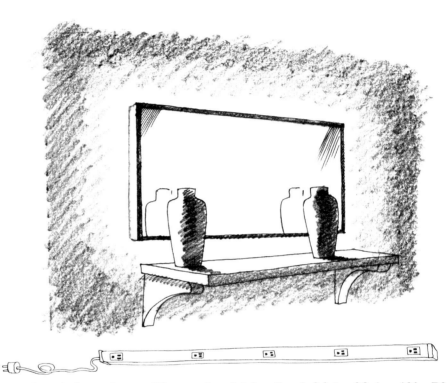

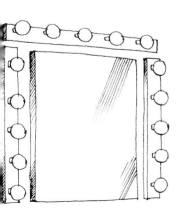

side of the mirror. These should be fixed 24 to 30 in. (61–76 cm) apart. They can be mounted on the wall with two screws per strip, and most strips have special keyholes for hanging. In these strips use white G16$\frac{1}{2}$ lamps in every outlet. This arrangement will give not only a theatrical effect but exactly the sort of light that theatrical makeup demands—which means good. The plug-in strips can also be disguised into the walls with paint.

An alternative is to use fluorescent fixtures in place of the plug-in strips—again down the sides of the mirror.

LIGHTING BEHIND THE MIRROR. A purely decorative effect can be made by positioning light behind a large mirror. To do this, mount the mirror 2$\frac{1}{2}$ to 3 in. (6–8 cm) from the wall on a frame recessed 3 to 4 in. (8–10 cm) from the mirror edge. Attach plug-in strips or fluorescent channels to the back of this frame; this will provide a soft halo of light.

Luminous ceiling fixtures General lighting can be provided with luminous ceiling fixtures. If they are to be functional they should be located over the counter or vanity unit and as close to the front of the counter as possible. They can be bought and fixed quite easily, or one can be improvised from a casement window frame suspended below lighting fixtures.

LIGHTING
ART AND
OBJECTS

Lighting Art and Objects

Paintings, prints, and drawings If you want to light a painting to its best advantage, get out the work light recommended in Chapter 3, "General Planning," and experiment with different angles to see what makes the best effect. With some paintings the direction of light makes very little difference, but others may have enough varnish on the surface so that light from certain angles either glances back into somebody's eyes or distorts the painting—sometimes to the extent of making the content disappear altogether.

Theoretically, lighting fixtures should be placed so that light hits the center of the painting at an angle of 30 degrees from the vertical. This should prevent reflections from the frame, glass, or surface of the picture, and also avoids shadows from the frame, specially thick paint texture, and so on. But for various practical reasons you might not always be able to use that angle—because of the shape of the room, or the position the painting has had to be hung in—and you should certainly check the normal sight lines of people seated or standing in the room to ensure that no unshielded light sources are in view.

One interesting point to remember is that artists usually paint by daylight indoors, and tend to favor painting by the light of a north window because north light does not change color as much as light from other parts of the sky (in the Southern Hemisphere painters naturally pick a south window). This light is bluer than the incandescent variety normally found in people's houses, and some museums and art galleries use extremely pale blue filters over incandescent bulbs to eliminate the yellowness and to approximate as closely as possible the light the painter was working with in the first place. This is certainly worth experimenting with at home as well.

"But what about fluorescent?" you might justifiably ask. "I thought some of those were supposed to 'blue down' colors a bit." And so they do—but it is impossible to aim fluorescent bulbs, so unless you use them in a picture light mounted right on the frame of the painting, an incandescent bulb is better—and definitely more flexible.

Do not forget, too, that if the major surfaces in the room are at all strongly colored, some of that color will be reflected onto the painting as well, and make sure that there isn't an excessive difference in brightness between the lighted painting and surrounding areas. Also, a very high level of illumination over a long period of time might cause deterioration of the paint surface.

Picture-lighting fixtures, or at least lights suitable for that purpose, come in a variety of shapes and sizes and prices from the familiar picture light itself to spotlights with shutters known as framing projectors (see glossary), which can exactly confine light to the area of the painting.

The advantages of the common picture light are that it is easily installed and maintained; however, its disadvantages are inclined to

Preceding page, left: An oval slit edged with steel in a landing wall frames a series of plexiglass cubes containing a bird sculpture as well as a rectangular vase of flowers on a plexiglass column, dramatically lit by a low-voltage spotlight in the ceiling.

Preceding page, right: A magnificent circular pane of glass, painted in the Art Nouveau manner, is set into a hall ceiling, lit from behind, and surrounded by a series of small spots which reflect like stars in the tinted glass to form another band of decoration. Interior and lighting design by Larry Durham.

Above: A track-mounted spotlight with "barn doors" for control of spill light and, below, the same light without the "barn doors." Available through Lighting Center

Top right: In a New York apartment designed by Joe D'Urso, track around the edge of the space allows maximum flexibility with spots to light art, plants, or just glossy walls. An articulated pin-up lamp lights a collection of stones on a side table to the right of the picture.

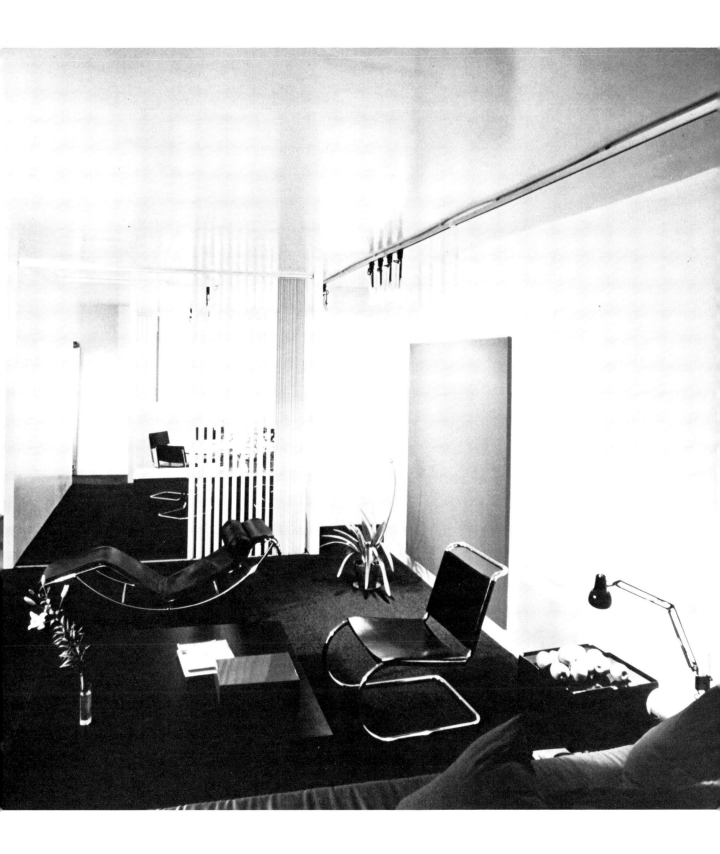

Left: Adjustable ceiling-mounted spots in a dark-walled hall light massed prints and drawings as well as a mirror which reflects back extra light. The white floor also gives good reflection.

Above: Track-mounted framing projectors from Lightolier.

Right: A pattern of downlights for "Ambient Luminescence" (see page 29).

outweigh its virtues: Unless you have an electric outlet just behind the painting you will have an unsightly cord showing, and, in any event, the light on top of the painting will be much brighter than the light at the bottom. If you choose the fluorescent variety, be sure to pick the correct color of bulb for the colors in the painting.

The next simplest form of lighting would be a downlight or downlights, whether mounted on or recessed into the ceiling, or fixed on a track. The advantages are the ease of controlling the amount of light on the painting, not only through a dimmer but also by means of different wattages of bulbs and the evenness of light that it is possible to project. The main disadvantage is that the beam from an ordinary downlight will form an elliptical shape on the wall so that you will be lighting parts of the wall as well as the painting itself. In this situation the area light becomes important enough to compete with the painting. The reverse of this method (and one that could certainly be used in rentals or in older houses where more obvious modern lighting might be obtrusive) would be to light from below with uplights or small spots concealed in urns or planters, on mantels or similar horizontal surfaces, or behind a sofa if it stands far enough away from the wall (but not if there will be traffic between the sofa and the wall).

Wallwashers fixed in much the same way as downlights (i.e. on track, or mounted on or recessed in the ceiling) or light fixtures concealed behind cornices or valances are best used when there are several paintings, prints, or drawings massed on the wall because they do light the entire area. The advantages are that pictures can be moved around and changed without having to readjust the lights. The disadvantages are a lack of contrast between the pictures and the surrounding wall and a lessening of any textural qualities that a painting might have.

Adjustable spots mounted in the same way can be trained on individual pictures, as can spots on "tree" or pole lights, but the most

satisfactory way (and the most complicated and expensive) is to use framing projectors, which with their use of lenses and shutters will allow the beam of light to fall only upon the painting. Its control can be very finely adjusted, usually to within a quarter of an inch or so.

Tapestries, macramé, rugs, and other textile wall hangings

If you bring your work light close and parallel to the wall to produce a so-called grazing light you will show up every irregularity, bump, and other defect in the surface. This is exactly how conscientious painters and plasterers finish their walls, and the fact that such a light emphasizes slight irregularities also means that it emphasizes the interesting textural effects that are natural to tapestries, macramé, rugs, and other highly worked surfaces. With some experimentation you will find the best angle, whether the light is almost directly overhead or otherwise. Again, fluorescent light will be of less use than incandescent because it does not throw the kind of light that results in the tiny highlights and shadows that potentially exist with every single thread or knot. This third dimension, however small, is a vital one for the full appreciation of fabrics and textures.

Sculpture (and other objects)

A sculpture is a three-dimensional object in space, and in lighting it the three-dimensional effect is all-important. The impact of any piece of sculpture depends absolutely on the interplay of light and shadow on it. Your work light should help you to see what angles of light make the sculpture and its

Left: Double inset track for quartz and low-voltage bulbs in this study designed by Ronald and Victoria Borus in collaboration with Ralph Bisdale. Track fixtures light objects and art; inset ceiling spots provide walk-through light.

Right: This splendid pewter Art Nouveau fireplace is grazed with light from high-hat downlights recessed into the ceiling above, and the raised peacock detail is picked out by the two inset wall lamps with their similar feeling. A Tiffany floor lamp at the side adds more accent lighting and picks out further detail on a screen behind.

shadows look most natural and interesting. If you want to cast "soft" shadows, simply establish the key light—whatever that might be—and then put another light in such a position that light is cast onto the primary shadow.

Clearly, the sculpture must be visible enough in all of its parts so that it is wholly understandable, and this will dictate whether you use several adjustable spots or just one, a floodlight or a framing projector, whether you boost it with uplight or not, or use uplight alone, and whether you use color filters or backlighting or both.

In fact, any object may be lit as though it were a piece of sculpture. Installing an adjustable fixture of some kind so that it is always ready to light a vase, an arrangement of flowers, a new plant, or a piece of interesting porcelain brings some useful variety to the lighting scheme and the room in general.

When you are attempting to light an entire collection massed in one area it is as important to experiment with the direction of light as to light individual objects. You can light collections arranged on shelves with overhead eyeball spots or strip lights concealed in front. The shadow on the shelf is not necessarily fatal to the appearance of the objects of the shelf below, although it is a good idea to put items on lower shelves as near the front edge as possible so that they will get the full benefit of the light.

Objects inside cabinets can be lit in another way with somewhat less punch or emphasis than from overhead spots. Use rows of tiny bulbs inset into Plugmold (see glossary) or miniature track, installed either along the front edge of each shelf or vertically along the sides of the cabinet. Either way, you must use equipment that will be hidden so as not to distract from the objects themselves.

Left: A collection of ancient and modern sculpture and other objects in room belonging to Van Day Truex is lighted very simply as befits its context (a simple hill house in Provence) by an ordinary pottery table lamp which only adds to the eclecticism, as does the inevitable light and shade.

Right: Uplights behind the plant and curtains add a subtle accent light to the candles in this dining room.

Page 124: A 15 w. bulb on a wall outlet mounting provides dramatic but economical lighting for the plant and head on this bench in architect Horace Gifford's own Manhattan apartment.

Page 125: All the photographs on this page show a neon chandelier in the black-glass-walled dining room designed by Ronald and Victoria Borus for David and Shelley Sutton. The neon glows red and blue, or just red, or just blue, and was devised by Ralph Bisdale. Incidentally, the shapes that seem like large white paintings hanging on the mirrored walls are actually spare leaves for the round table to make it enormously larger.

Page 126: (Top) Another light painting by Ralph Bisdale. (Center) Red fluorescent light mixed with blue (to take the sting out of the red) is combined with incandescent lamps more for illusion than anything else in Seymour d'Avigdor's brilliantly lit apartment. (Bottom) In lighting designer Ralph Bisdale's own hallway, light paintings are projected onto the wall in different abstract designs. Sliding light panels by the doorway are serviced by concealed fluorescent tubes in a blue color, and different effects can be achieved by moving the panels slightly. Photograph on page 126 by Charles Tracy.

Page 127: Decorative lighting by Ralph Bisdale, who has achieved this light painting with a galaxy of framing projectors and colored filters. Photograph by Tim Harden.

Page 128: Beams are studded with small white bulbs to dazzling effect in this holiday house on Fire Island.

Bottom left: Disco lighting by Ralph Bisdale with colored patterns projected onto the wall through rotating lenses and filters.

Bottom right: A Lalique glass lamp on a glass table is lit from underneath by a blue filtered uplight to ethereal effect in Seymour d'Avigdor's apartment, and a flashlight is used like a candle. Photograph by Tim Harden.

LIGHT & INDOOR PLANTS

Light and Indoor Plants

If books furnish a room, so do plants, and they go a long way toward giving any space personality as well as freshness. Careful accent lighting will imbue them with even more interest at night, revealing structure and casting shadows.

Light for the plant's own good Careful lighting will also give a boost to daylight, enhance plant growth, and make up for the changes from their natural habitat. Lighting conditions vary tremendously within the tropical belt, ranging from the dim green light of dense tropical jungles to the strong sunlight and seasonal rains of the sparsely treed open grasslands. Since the plants and indoor trees we buy for our homes come from such disparate light conditions it is important to try to understand the lighting requirements they grew up with and to emulate them as nearly as possible.

What is cheering to know is that, given the right kind and amount of artificial light, it should be quite possible to maintain healthy plants in spaces almost totally devoid of natural light. Plants do not need a vast amount of light for survival, but they do need a certain minimum amount in order to grow, and there is a great difference between a barely surviving plant—which is all too common—and a healthy growing one. Interestingly, the natural light in a room might *seem* enough, but it is often only enough to keep the plant alive, and very far from enough to help it push out new leaves. If you know the exact amount of light that any given plant needs, you can give it a boost by setting up a few bulbs or fluorescent tubes or a proper "grow bulb" in areas where you would like plant growth. Later in this chapter we give a table, taken from Rex E. Mabe's *Gardening with Lights,* listing most varieties of houseplants and the approximate minimum light needed for their good health—which can, in fact, be boosted up so that they reach maximum, bursting health. But before this list can make any real sense you will need to know how to measure the natural light you have, and how much artificial light you will need to supplement it for satisfactory results. (Incidentally, *Gardening with Lights* provided a good deal of useful information for this chapter and is a valuable book for anyone with a particular interest in the subject. It is available for $1.50 from Potpourri Press, P.O. Box 10312, Greensboro, N.C. 27404.)

Photographers need to measure the amount of light falling on their subject so they can choose an appropriate lens opening and exposure time for taking their shots. This can be done directly, by means of a light meter, which measures the light—in foot-candles or lux—falling on a given point; or it can be done indirectly, but more conveniently, by using an exposure meter, often incorporated into the camera mechanism. A foot-candle, as explained in the glossary, is the amount of light falling on one square foot of surface located one foot away from a candle in a dark room, and this foot-candle measurement

is also used in our list (multiply by ten for an approximate equivalent in lux). Many plants will just about survive in an area where the light is only 10 foot-candles strong, but if there were 100 foot-candles those plants would grow and flourish out of all recognition.

Now, a 40 w. incandescent bulb produces 70 foot-candles of light when it is measured 1 ft./30 cm from the bulb—if, that is, the light is directed mainly in one direction with a reflector shade. The same bulb with the same reflector shade will produce only 20 foot-candles of light at a distance of 2 ft./61 cm; if that bulb is used in a fixture that allows light to spill out in all directions, its intensity will be reduced to only 9 foot-candles at 3 ft./91 cm. All this is to prove that the amount of light a plant receives depends on its distance from a light source, and you can find out how much light any given plant is receiving at any given time by using a photographer's light meter.

To do this, the area where the light is to be measured should be covered with a piece of clean, thick white paper about 2 ft./61 cm square, placed so that it faces in the direction the light comes from. If you are measuring both natural and artificial light, the paper should be directed toward the strongest light source, whether bulb or window, and at the level where the plant's leaves would be. In the case of a tall plant, fix the paper at a level equal to about two-thirds of its height if it were standing there. When the paper is in place, set the ASA film speed index on the camera or exposure meter at 200; set the shutter speed at $1/125$ of a second; aim the light meter at the paper, making sure that it "sees" only the white paper and that no shadow is being cast, and you will get a reading that suggests the proper lens opening to use if you were taking a picture. This reading is called the "f-stop," and can be used with a chart that comes with the light meter to find how many foot-candles of light are available. For example, if the reading is f4, you are getting about 64 foot-candles; f8, about 250 foot-candles; f16, about 1,000 foot-candles.

A light meter will show you the *exact* amount of light a plant is getting, but you can get a good rough idea of its light ration by looking at the plant itself. If the stems are getting elongated and the leaves unnaturally weedy, it is being starved of light. If the stems are very short and the leaves seem to be hugging the pot, then the plant is getting too much light.

Below we have listed four categories of plants according to how much light they need ("light situations"): those needing only 50–100 foot-candles, those needing 100–200, those needing 200–300, and those needing 600–1,400 foot-candles and up. First, to help you position your plants better for natural light we have listed which exposures will provide what amounts of natural light (in foot-candles).

YOU CAN EXPECT 50–100 FOOT-CANDLES OF LIGHT ON AVERAGE:

- *If a plant is placed directly in front of a north window that has most of the sky blocked by trees, buildings, or other obstructions.*
- *If a plant is placed a few feet away or just to the side of a north window that is not obstructed.*
- *If a plant is placed a few feet away from an east or west window that has most of the sky obstructed in some way.*
- *If a plant is placed 8 ft./2.4 m back from, or 2 ft./61 cm to the side of, an east or west window that is unobstructed.*
- *If a plant is placed 10 ft./3 m back from, or a few feet to either side of, a south window that has most of the sky obstructed.*
- *If a plant is placed 10 to 15 ft. (3–4.6 m) back from, or 5 ft./1.5 m to the side of, a south window that is not obstructed.*

YOU CAN EXPECT 100–200 FOOT-CANDLES ON AVERAGE:

- *If a plant is placed directly in front of a north window that is unobstructed.*
- *If a plant is placed directly in front of an east or west window that has about half the sky obstructed in some way*
- *If a plant is placed 10 ft./3 m back from, or 2 to 3 ft. (61–91 cm) to the side of, a south window when the sky is partially obstructed.*

YOU CAN EXPECT 200–300 FOOT-CANDLES ON AVERAGE:

- *If a plant is placed directly in front of an unobstructed east or west window.*
- *If a plant is placed directly in front of a south window that has half the sky obstructed.*
- *If a plant is placed 5 ft./1.5 m back from, or 2 to 3 ft. (61–91 cm) to the side of, an unobstructed south window.*

YOU CAN EXPECT UP TO 1,500 FOOT-CANDLES ON AVERAGE:

- *If the direct rays of the sun are falling on most or all of the leaves of a plant.*
- *Sometimes there is much more than 1,500 and sometimes much less, but this foot-candle rating is an average, and would be sufficient light for the most demanding house plant if the light is available three to four hours a day.*

Right: Grow lights are recessed behind the ceiling above the plants in this striking interior designed by architects Louis Muller and William Murphy. Photographed by Mark Ross.

MINIMUM LIGHT NEEDED FOR DIFFERENT PLANTS

Although the following plants will grow in the light situations listed, they will do much better if the amount of foot-candles is doubled or tripled. This applies especially to the blooming plants, cacti, and succulents listed in light situation no. 3.

Light situation no. 1   (50–100 foot-candles)

- Aspidistra
- Bamboo palm
- Chinese evergreen
- Cissus
- Dracaenas:
  cinta

(Pleomela
gracilis)
Warneckii
Sanderana
Sanderana
Godseffiana
- Fatshedera

- Ferns of all types
  except asparagus
- Ivy
- Kentia palm
- Miniature palm
- Nephthytis
  (Syngonium

podophyllum)
- Philodendrons:
  cordatum
  pertusum
  (Monstera
  deliciosa)

Selloum
snake plant
(sansevieria)
- Scindapsus
- Spathiphyllum

Light situation no. 2   (100–200 foot-candles)
All plants listed in light situation no. 1, plus:

- Dracaenas:
  Marginata
  Massangeana
- Fatsia japonica
- Ficus:
  lyrata

elastica
- Maranta leuconeura
  (prayer plant)
- Piggyback plant
  (Tolmiea
  Menziesii)

- Peperomia
- Plectranthus
  (Swedish ivy,
  Swedish begonia)
- Pony tail
  (Beaucarnea

recurvata)
- Pothos
- Rhapis palm
- Saxifraga sarmentosa
- Schefflera
- Wandering Jew

Light situation no. 3   (200–300 foot-candles)
All plants listed in light situations nos. 1 and 2, plus:

- Aeschynanthus
  (lipstick plant)
- Abutilon*
- African violet
- Asparagus ferns*
- Begonias
- Bromeliads*
- Cacti*

- Chlorophytum
  comosum
  (air plant,
  spider ivy)*
- Clerodendrum*
- Coleus*
- Columnea*
- Cyclamen

- Dieffenbachia
- Fittonia
- Fuchsia
- Forced bulbs
- Gloxinia
- Helxine*
- Herbs*

- Jade plant*
- Kalanchoe*
- Orchids*
- Pilea Cadierei
  (aluminum plant)
- Selaginella*
- Succulents*
- Zebra plant*

*May also be
grown in light
situation no. 4)

Light situation no. 4   (600–1,400 foot-candles and up)
All plants listed under light situation no. 3 that are designated with an asterisk (*), plus:

- Aralia
  dizygotheca
  polyscias (ming)
- Areca palm
- Bougainvillea
- Citrus:
  calamondin

lime
lemon
orange
- Croton
- Crown-of-thorns
  (Euphorbia Milii)

- Cycas
- Dipladenia
- Geraniums
- Hibiscus
- Hoya
- Norfolk Island pine

(Araucaria
heterophylla)
- Phoenix palm
  (date palm)
- Podocarpus
- Sedums
- Yucca

Once you have a good idea of what natural light your plants get, you can figure out how to improve the situation with artificial lights, especially "grow lights"—incandescent bulbs or fluorescent tubes that can duplicate the rays of the sun. Theoretically, any artificial light is potentially a grow light, but some forms are considerably bet-

Right: In Ed Apea's apartment in New York City the clever handling of light, mirror, and different levels makes the best possible use of the given space. Plants are lit by an uplight underneath and by an angled spot from the track above. Photograph by Michael Datoli.

ter than others. The necessary rays for plant growth are blue, red, and infrared. Regular incandescent light bulbs deliver red and infrared rays, and regular fluorescent tubes produce red and blue rays, so a combination of the two—especially three parts fluorescent to one part incandescent (by wattage)—makes a perfect light condition for plant growth.

However, not many people have the room—or the money—to install all these special fixtures. This is where grow lights come in. They are not as ideal as the three-to-one combination, but they are better than either incandescent or fluorescent lights on their own (and of these, fluorescents followed by mercury-vapor bulbs [see glossary] are better than incandescents, which can be too hot).

These special grow lights were first manufactured by Sylvania and became available in the early 1960s as a type of fluorescent tube called Gro-Lux. Soon after, Westinghouse brought out a similar fluorescent tube called Plant-gro, and since then other manufacturers such as General Electric have experimented with the same sort of

Above: Plants are massed on the bench and low table and around the window area in an apartment designed by architects William Muller and Louis Murphy. They are lit by a mixture of low pendant lighting and spots from a track above, and doubled in the wall of mirror to the right, which in any case doubles the apparent size of a narrow room.

principles, and special trays and stands were developed for using them. They were actually developed to screen out yellow and green rays normally produced by fluorescent lights but not necessary for plant growth, and to concentrate on the red and blue rays that were. They work better than regular fluorescent or incandescent lights used on their own, especially for flowering plants, which need more energy for growing than the plain-foliage variety; they are available in various watt sizes and lengths, and they fit into any regular fluorescent fixture. The great thing is that with a couple of these you could grow plants in rooms with no natural light at all.

Since the beginning of the 1970s there have also been a number of attempts at incandescent grow lights in which manufacturers have tried to introduce more blue rays into the lighting source. They are not as good as the fluorescent variety, but they are better than ordinary fluorescent tubes, although you must remember not to use them too close to plants or they will scorch the leaves.

Here is a table of the amount of booster light to be expected at distances of 1 ft./30 cm and 2 ft./61 cm from fluorescent and incandescent bulbs. Grow lights produce approximately the same foot-candles by wattage as the regular bulbs, only the quality of their light is different.

FLUORESCENT LIGHTING

Simple fluorescent fixtures without reflectors generally hold from one to four tubes. These tubes are usually 40 w. size and were used for the following light measurements.

Wattage	Distance in Ft./Cm	Foot-candles
1—40	1/30	120
1—40	2/61	75
2—40	1/30	240
2—40	2/61	100
3—40	1/30	360
3—40	2/61	140
4—40	1/30	480
4—40	2/61	190

INCANDESCENT LIGHTING

Incandescent bulbs of the wattages listed below, when used with a simple photographer's reflector, would produce the following light measurements:

Wattage	Distance in Ft./Cm	Foot-candles
40	1/30	70
40	2/61	20
60	1/30	95
60	2/61	30
75	1/30	145
75	2/61	45
100	1/30	205
100	2/61	55
150	1/30	2705
150	2/61	90

(Note: High-wattage spotlights should not be used closer to the foliage on a plant than 3 ft./61 cm.)

Like people, plants should have a period of darkness every day as well, otherwise they will wear themselves out with all the growing, and since 16 hours illumination a day is considered healthy for foliage plants, it follows that 8 hours in the dark is equally good for them. Flowering plants in general might do better with more, with the exception of African violets and gloxinias, which like as much light in the 24 hours as is possible.

Lighting plants for effect   Lighting plants for aesthetic rather than practical reasons is a different matter altogether. Lighting that enhances the appearance of a plant is not necessarily the sort of light that is best for making it grow. We have already mentioned that light sources, particularly incandescent, should not be placed too near to foliage; bearing this in mind, the following methods of lighting are all effective in their way:

1. *Recess, surface-mount, or suspend incandescent downlights well above the plant or plants so that the light bounces through the leaves.*

2. *Place plants underneath a luminous panel or soffit (see Chapter 6, "Do-It-Yourself Ideas") using fluorescent or incandescent bulbs.*

3. *Silhouette plants by standing them in front of a luminous wall panel, a light-washed wall, or concealed uplights.*

4. *Recess lights right into the earth to provide subtle uplight.*

5. *Put plants in a special planting rack containing regular fluorescent and incandescent bulbs in the proportion mentioned on page 140, or just incandescent alone, or with special fluorescent or incandescent grow lights.*

Remember that all plants tend to grow toward the light. This should be kept in mind when locating equipment.

Left: Lytetiles by Lightolier: ceiling fixtures of polished metal with small fluorescent tubes attached. These may be left bare or covered with linen squares.

Right: A dramatic tunnel of plants and light and metropolitan view in architect Horace Gifford's own New York apartment. The glass enclosure is reflected indefinitely by mirror, which equally reflects the plants lit by uplights from the trough installed below them.

OUTDOOR
LIGHTING

Outdoor
Lighting Lighting up the outside of a house—or a garden or yard, a terrace or a porch—has several purposes, among which are identification, safety and security, and the strictly ornamental. The two main things to remember are that at night what is not lit is to all intents and purposes invisible; and that ill-considered lighting can cause disturbing contrasts of brightness and darkness. Luckily, eyes adapt fairly quickly to the dark, so that quite low levels of illumination outside are sufficient to see by. Whatever the level, careful shielding of some sort should always be used to prevent glare. And outdoor illumination looks much more natural if light sources are hidden and the light is reflected from walls, trees, or shrubs.

Lighted house numbers, visible from the street, are thoughtful courtesies. Doorways, porches, and keyholes should be lit up to make it easy for people to let themselves in and out, and to make it equally easy to identify callers, as well as to deter prowlers. But do avoid clear-glass fixtures and exposed high-wattage bulbs that might be visible to passing drivers, which could give an after-image and cause accidents. Steps should be well lit, with attention to both treads and risers; walkways and paths should be easy to see along; and any obstacles should be well illuminated.

When there is any sort of garden or yard spreading away from the house you can light up the perimeters to create a feeling of enclosure. To emphasize the relationship between the house and the grounds it is set in there should be some lit feature or features right outside—whether a path, a group of shrubs or flower beds, or whatever there is to light.

If you are lighting for effect—as opposed to safety, which you should provide anyway—the inside of the house should somehow be visually related to the outside. On a fine night, a large window with no curtains or shutters, or with the curtains or shutters drawn back, can

Preceding page, left: An Ingo Maurer fan light for George Kovacs is a weird and wonderful sight stuck in the earth among the trees. Photograph by Christof Piepenstock.

Preceding page, right: This house is so much of glass that the interior light spilling out is quite enough to light the outside as well.

Right: In this London house, brick piers down the façade of the building are grazed with light from downlights which also light up the front door. Large outdoor lights illumine a bed of foliage and the cobbled yard, and flowerpots and an urn stand out in sharp relief against light pouring from windows and door, so that both house and its immediate surrounds seem related and continuous.

Below left: Contemporary exterior brackets light up and down.

Below right: Traditional lanterns flank a doorway.

Left: A fluorescent fixture casts a floo
of light along a garden path.

Right: A portable outdoor PAR 38
spot, with a spike for easy fixing and
flexible lead, picks out the statue amon
the background foliage. The front of the
lamp is green (other colors are available). Photograph from Concord
Lighting (G.B.).

Below: A simple outdoor fixture with
spike conceals a PAR bulb. It can be
stuck right into the earth among plants

seem like an uncomfortable dark "hole" unless you have some sort of exterior vista (quite apart from the mirror effect that is often created on the glass, with the reflection of the interior jumbling up with any objects immediately outside like garden chairs or flowerpots). In this case, use a dimmer to lower the level of light in the room and balance it with exterior light to the point where the reflections will vanish.

If you light the floor of the patio or yard or terrace that is just outside, you at least provide some sort of continuity with the inside floor, but you should also light a vertical surface: a wall, a line of shrubs, a hedge. And it would be a waste not to take advantage of the sort of effects that can be achieved with artificial light that are simply not possible in daylight: uplight shining into trees, light grazing an urn and revealing its detail, the silhouette of a finely shaped shrub, a combination of uplight and downlight glancing through a mass of foliage, the glow of ornamental water and swimming pools.

When you light the façade of a house, it is interesting how far a little light will go. Often the spill of light reflected from trees, or from fixtures meant to light pathways and steps, is more than enough not only to distinguish the main features of a building but the details as well, and of course one is always attracted to any light seen coming from the inside, whether it is glowing through curtains or blinds or revealing a glimpse of the interior. But if the house is built of a material you would like to emphasize, place one or two 75 w. PAR 38 bulbs in fixtures 2 to 3 ft. (61–91cm) from the building to graze across the wall. The fixtures should be concealed, if possible, in the grass or a flower bed or some sort of greenery. This way the light will show up the texture of the wall as well as delineating the building itself, throwing light up to the eaves and into any adjacent trees. But do be careful to consider any neighbors by making sure that they are not disturbed by the beam of light.

Outdoor equipment Outdoor lighting equipment obviously has to meet certain criteria. It has to be moisture-proof and occasionally submersible (as for pool lighting) and certainly weathertight so that rain, snow, mud, dust, or extremes of temperature will not affect it. It should be built of a noncorroding material, and should only be con-

nected through a ground fault interrupter that can turn off the electricity, in case of defective equipment or an accidental grounding, before anyone can get a shock. This sort of safety problem can best be avoided by using low-voltage equipment, particularly in a small garden, or when lighting low shrubs or the façade of an average-size house, and especially when there are small children.

However, *the most versatile piece of equipment is the PAR 38 bulb itself.* It can be turned on while covered with snow or ice and won't break (in contrast to an ordinary A bulb, which will often shatter if a few drops of water splash onto it while it is hot). It is available as a flood or spot, in 75 or 150 w. sizes, and even for a 12-volt current supply. A simple holder like the one illustrated at right includes a large gasket to make the assembly weatherproof when the lamp is screwed in; you can stick it in the earth or (by detaching the spike) mount it on an outlet box; it allows you to try out and aim the light as needed; and a number of accessories such as glare shields, color filters, and so on are generally available. It should be placed so that it is hidden from most viewing angles and concealed with stones, bricks, low shrubs, logs, or whatever is available. There are also colored PAR bulbs with weatherproof faces in highly saturated blue, red, green, amber, yellow, and pink. The warm colors look rather unnatural out of doors, but the blue can be nicely mysterious if mystery is wanted.

The exact wattage, and whether you need a flood or a spot bulb, can best be decided by experimenting; wattage will depend partly on how many fixtures you are intending to use, since more than one will be necessary for certain effects. For example, a tree in full blossom might best be shown off by locating a 150 w. PAR 38 spot bulb 50 ft./ 15 m from the trunk and aimed at the top of the tree, with a PAR 38 flood placed only 3 ft./91 cm from the trunk and aimed directly upward through the spread of branches.

There are other fixtures specifically designed for use with low-wattage 12-volt bulbs, which have the advantage of being economical, safe to handle, and easy to install. A typical kit includes fixtures with bulbs, detachable spikes, clips on the fixtures to enable you to connect them easily at any point along the wire, and a transformer that can be plugged into any outlet.

Some fixtures can actually be buried right in the earth. The bulb is protected either by a lens or louver, and they are sometimes entirely submersible and able to operate while actually underwater in pools, or when drenched by rain, hosings, sprinklers, and so on. Others need to be installed so as to allow water to drain away, so it is important to check the manufacturers' recommendations. In any case, both kinds are very inconspicuous and especially useful when you want light coming from the middle of a smooth lawn or an area of paving where an ordinary fixture would look too obtrusive.

Light from buried fixtures can be aimed at an angle as well as

This uplight buried in the earth is inconspicuous (cutaway view).

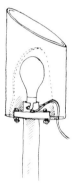

Cutaway view of a low-voltage uplight that is easy to make at home.

A low-voltage adjustable fixture with spike planted in the earth.

Above: This house is literally outlined with light, which splashes onto the
terrace below and merges with light
spilling from the long windows, as well
as grazing the brick wall behind. The
effect is achieved with recessed downlights (in this case, Multigroove) spaced
under the overhang of the tiled roof.
Photograph from Concord Lighting.

Perforated housing creates a myriad
twinkles for an outdoor "Play of
Brilliants" (see page 31).

straight up, either by tilting the entire fixture itself, or by tilting the
bulb when the fixture is made that way, or both. The disadvantage of
these buriable fixtures is that fixture and wiring together are much
more expensive than others we have mentioned. But you invariably
have to pay more for the ideal.

Apart from this group of incandescent bulbs and equipment, you
can also get *mercury-vapor bulbs and equipment* with roughly similar functions. Of course, they do last much longer, are cheap to run,
and give out a higher output of light per watt, but these advantages
are offset by lack of flexibility, the fact that each bulb size needs its
own ballast so you can't interchange bulbs, and their color. Their
green cast is flattering to foliage and to some blue flowers, but it is
unpleasant on stone, brick, warm-colored flowers (red, yellow,
orange, and pink), and it looks quite ghastly on human complexions.
Since they are exceptionally long-lasting, their best use would be in a
position that is difficult to get at (like the top of a tree).

Fluorescent uplights can be useful under large shrubs or groups of
shrubs, but they produce a rather hazy effect, with no clear modeling
of leaf or trunk, and they cannot really be directed. If you want to see
exactly the sort of light they give, hold a piece of tracing paper over
an incandescent uplight, shielding your eyes so you don't see the
brightness of the paper. If you like this rather diffuse light, they can be
useful and cheap to run, but *incandescent uplights* are more generally
useful outside, since they can be aimed properly and, in fact, usually
do a lot more than just illuminate what they are aimed at. If you aim
an incandescent uplight onto a wall, light will be reflected from the

Left: Note the flood of light from this fluorescent outdoor uplight with spikes.

Below: A sketch of the homemade candlelight in a waxed-paper bag described on this page.

Top right: Recessed Multigroove downlights edge the perimeter of this house in Zurich, Switzerland, giving dramatic focus to the house as well as acting as a deterrent to prowlers.

Bottom right: A few of the exterior lanterns currently available. They are all made by Lightolier.

wall back onto the adjacent path. Similarly, light shining up into a broad-leafed tree will be reflected back down to the surrounding area; it could thus, in effect, be lighting steps, or a path, or a flower bed as well.

Some of the nicest kinds of outdoor lighting are *small flares or potted candlelights* indicating paths, steps, turning points, and so on at ground level—rather like miniature versions of the taxiing lights on airport runways. You can make these yourself by buying waxed-paper bags about 8 in./20 cm across, cutting ¼ in./6 mm holes in them, filling them with about 3 in./7 cm of dry sand or earth, jiggling them around so they stay steady, and centering candles firmly down the middle. Another version of this "play of brilliants" that Richard Kelly defined (see Chapter 3, "General Planning") would be to strew small bare bulbs like Christmas-tree lights in beds of ground cover like periwinkles or ivy or pachysandra; or to string them around trees or bushes.

Lighting from above If you decide that you want to use a fixture or fixtures that light from above you must also decide if you want the fixture to be a beacon (i.e. "the driveway starts here" sort of light) or a light giver (the "look at the color of this azalea" variety). There are all sorts of fixtures for both purposes on the market, and some that combine the two. They may distribute light either symmetrically all around, or more in one direction than another, and are made to accept a variety of incandescent, fluorescent, and mercury-vapor bulbs (see illustrations). It is evident that the higher you put your light source the more area it can cover effectively; but you still must choose between a beacon and a light giver. A traditionally styled lantern can deliver as much light as you need. It will also produce glare, but glare from about 8 ft./2.4 m or more above the ground is easier to tolerate than glare at or below eye level.

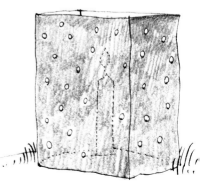

Lighting trees Hanging a fixture from a tree or fastening it onto a branch or high on the trunk frees you from the difficulties of installing a tall post (with the attendant chores of buried wiring, foundations for the post, etc.) and makes possible a variety of downlighting effects. Here again experimentation is useful. Try out the location of the fixture and its aiming angle. The ordinary pressed-glass PAR 38 bulb should be used, and the 150 w. flood is the best to try first for use from heights of about 10 to 18 ft. (3.1–5.5 m); above that height you will need spotlights or several floodlights.

Combining uplighting into the tree foliage with downlighting results in fascinating effects. Also, if a tree is "opaque," with a closely knit foliage structure, try to locate your light so that it grazes along the full length of the tree form. More than one fixture will probably be necessary, fitted with spots rather than floods, to reach to the top.

If a tree is more "transparent," like a fruit tree in blossom, for example, light the tree from inside. Use a flood bulb, 3 to 6 ft. (91–182 cm) from the trunk and shining upward, and see that it is far enough away from the trunk so that the foliage and blossoms, rather than the trunk, assume importance.

Left: A little light goes a long way outside at night. The green light under this tree not only illuminates the foliage but casts a good light on the façade of the house as well. Photograph by John Watson, Landscape Illuminator.

Right: A low-level combination light-giver and beacon by Atelier International.

Lighting water The most effective light for a *fountain* is from a point in the water directly below the area on which the spray is falling. Suspend or put the face of the lamp 3 in./7 cm below the water and try to train it along the actual fall of the spray.

Swimming pools are almost always painted a very light blue so that they will look clean and inviting. Just one or two waterproof fixtures recessed into or fixed to the side walls of a pool will give it a very inviting glow at night. Light from overhead—as, for example, from an overhanging tree down onto the surface of the water—is not as successful in giving the same glow. Lights in the pool are also more comfortable than overhead lights for nocturnal swimmers.

Ponds, streams, and ornamental pools also look more natural with light from the side. Conceal fixtures in long grass, rushes, or wildflowers along the banks.

Note, though, that U.S. and most other national electrical codes are strict on wiring for lighting fixtures or receptacles near water out of doors; this includes both permanent and storable swimming pools or ornamental pools. You are specifically restricted to certain combinations of horizontal and vertical distance from the water (protecting you of course from touching the water and the electrical outlet simultaneously). It would be most unwise to install any electrical equipment within 16 ft./4.9 m of any kind of pool without at least having a licensed electrician check the installation for you.

Top left: A couple of waterproof fixtures are recessed into the side of this games-room pool. Square downlights located quite near the walls light up the collection of rugs and are fixed over the billiard table. They also highlight the texture of the white-painted stone walls.

Bottom left: Recessed Multigroove downlights mixed with wallwashers to accent screen and sculpture make this indoor pool seem very splendid. Special chlorine-proof fixtures line the side of the pool under the water. Note that the downlights only light up the surrounds of the pool. Light over the water would be too disturbing for swimmers.

Top right: The surrounds of this London pool are lit by recessed Multigroove downlights with special chlorine-proof sleeves over PAR 38 bulbs. More fixtures are recessed into the sides of the pool itself. All three photographs from Concord Lighting.

Bottom right: This sketch shows the sort of simple submersible fixture that is available for underwater lighting. It makes the water surface seem to glow.

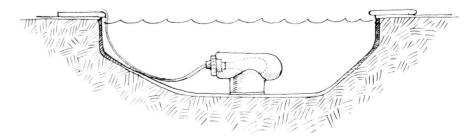

SOME ENERGY SAVING IDEAS

Some Energy Saving Ideas

Normally, lighting accounts for only about 16 percent of electricity bills, but the opportunities for genuine, worthwhile savings in energy still exist. In fact, as part of the national effort to save energy, each American state either has, or by law shortly will have, an energy code that includes a statement on how much electricity may be used for lighting alone. Each state is free to develop its own set of standards—and you should check how your locality is affected—but most follow the guidelines developed by the American Society of Heating, Refrigeration, and Air-Conditioning Engineers (ASHRAE). The parts of this code affecting the use of electricity for lighting only apply to bathrooms, kitchens, and laundries; the amounts allocated as upper limits are shown in the tables on page 163.

But energy codes aside, you have to understand how ordinary light bulbs are rated before you can choose the most efficient and energy-saving lighting. Ratings now appear on the sleeves or jackets in which bulbs are packaged and are categorized like this:

- *Watts: As we have noted in the glossary, this measures the amount of electricity used by the bulb.*

- *Lumens: This measures the actual amount of light produced by the bulb; the lumen output is noted on the sleeve in terms of average initial lumens.*

- *Bulb life: A bulb will burn for only a certain length of time; the sleeve in which it is packaged will give the average number of hours of use you can expect from it before it burns out.*

"Long-life" or "extended service" bulbs are designed to last longer than standard bulbs, but, as happens invariably with incandescent bulbs, the longer the life, the less light is produced. For example, a standard 100 w. bulb will give some 750 hours of use while producing 1,750 lumens. A long-life 100 w. bulb might last up to three times as long, but it will produce an average of only about 80 percent of the light of the standard bulb for the same amount of electricity. Therefore, the best way to use long-life bulbs is in locations that are difficult to get at–like very high ceilings and ceilings above stairwells.

Here are some suggestions designed to save energy by using the right bulb for the job:

Look at the rating on a bulb sleeve to see the average initial lumens. If you are choosing between two 100 w. bulbs, choose the one delivering the most lumens and you will get more light for the same amount of electricity.

When practical, use one higher-wattage bulb where you are now using several lower-wattage bulbs. One 100 w. incandescent bulb produces nearly twice as much light as four 25 w. bulbs and costs about a quarter as much as the four together.

Consider fluorescent lighting, because it has a number of energy-saving advantages. Fluorescent bulbs are much more efficient than incandescent bulbs. Lumen for lumen they use as much as two-thirds

Preceding pages: Examples of designer Ingo Maurer's "bulb clear" lamps designed in 1966 for George Kovacs. Photographed in a still life with herbs and vegetables, they seem appropriately self-sufficient for the frontispiece of a chapter on saving energy. Photograph by Christof Piepenstock.

Above, left to right: The many forms of task-lighting fixtures: adjustable table lamps; a clip-on light; a low-voltage track fixture designed by Ralph Bisdale (available from Ad Hoc Housewares, 842 Lexington Avenue, New York City); and a silvered-bowl track fixture from Lightolier for spot-on light, since this variety can be very carefully aimed.

less energy; they last up to twenty times longer; and they can usually be used anywhere that you do not need to control the direction of the light. But do remember to choose the right color bulbs for domestic uses (for recommendations see glossary and Chapter 2, "Some Common Questions and Answers").

For reading, writing, playing the piano, or any activity where you need to be able to direct the light to a particular spot, try to use reflector bulbs. As we have explained in the glossary, they are designed to direct the light in a controlled beam in a specific direction. With standard bulbs a lot of the light produced is trapped in the lighting fixture or within the shade. In fact, 50 w. R20 bulb (or 60 w. in U.K.) may often directly substitute for an ordinary 100 w. bulb.

Use three-way bulbs in conventional table or floor lamps. These give a choice of settings, with the highest setting for use when you really need it.

Dimmers give enormous flexibility in using higher-wattage bulbs, since they actually conserve electricity while allowing easy changes in the mood and tone of a room. Moreover, bulbs last a good deal longer if they are kept dimmed—even if only slightly.

If you use night lights, there are some available now that take only 4 watts instead of the previous 7 watts, and have a longer-rated life than the older versions. This 3 watt difference may not seem much, but considering that night lights are usually left on for long periods, or even all the time, the electricity saved can be considerable.

In order to make it easy to turn off lights you don't need, put switches where they are easy to see and reach, and provide them at every exit.

Bulbs of any kind must be kept clean if you are to get maximum light output. Dirty or blackened bulbs use the same amount of electricity as clean new ones and give far less light. You will also get the most from your bulbs if room surfaces are light-colored or white.

For outside lights consider using mercury-vapor bulbs. They are

more than twice as efficient as incandescents and last over ten times longer. A 40 w. "de luxe white" mercury-vapor bulb produces 1,350 lumens compared with 455 lumens for a 40 w. incandescent. If the color is objectionable—and it must be said that it certainly is not flattering to the complexion nor to most colors—consider the low-wattage PAR bulbs now available in 55, 75, and 100 w. versions. Also, put outdoor lighting on a timer or a dusk-to-dawn photocell so that the whole system is automatic and not dependent on someone remembering to switch it on or off.

KITCHENS

ROOM DIMENSIONS		POWER BUDGET
Width ft. (m)	Length ft. (m)	(watts)
4 (1.2)	4–12 (1.2–3.7)	280
5 (1.5)	5–11 (1.5–3.4)	280
	12 & over (3.5 & over)	320
6 (1.8)	6–9 (1.8–2.7)	280
	10–12 (3.0–3.7)	320
	13 & over (4 & over)	360
7 (2.1)	7–8 (2.1–2.4)	280
	9–10 (2.7–3.0)	320
	11–14 (3.4–4.3)	360
	15 & over (4.6 & over)	400
8 (2.4)	8–9 (2.4–2.7)	320
	10–11 (3.0–3.4)	360
	12 & over (3.7 & over)	400
9 (2.7)	9–11 (2.7–3.4)	360
	12 & over (3.7 & over)	400
10 & over (3.0 & over)	10–11 (3.0–3.4)	360
	12 & over (3.7 & over)	400

BATHROOMS

ROOM DIMENSIONS		POWER BUDGET	
Width ft. (m)	Length ft. (m)	For one grooming location (watts)	For two grooming location (watts)
5 (1.5)	6–7 (1.8–2.1)	130	195
5 (1.5)	8–10 (2.4–3.0)	160	225
6 (1.8)	6–8 (1.8–24)	160	225
6 (1.8)	9–10 (2.7–3.0)	200	265
7 (2.1)	7 (2.1)	160	225
7 (2.1)	8–10 (2.4–3.0)	200	265

Left: The floor lamp here with its three-way switch in Doreen Chu's Manhattan apartment reflects its light on the aluminum slats of the vertical blind behind that catches and refracts it, giving double the light and more for the energy output.

Right: No architect's drafting board is complete without an articulated swiveling lamp like this one by Luxo.

Overleaf: A still life of Ingo Maurer's fan lights in all their variety. They are available through George Kovacs Lighting. Photograph by Christof Piepenstock.

An A to Z of Lighting Terms

(Note: Every term used to help explain another term is itself explained somewhere in this glossary. For cross-referencing purposes these terms will be found in *italics.*)

"A" BULB: The most commonly used bulb shape; known in the U.K. as a "GLS" (general lighting service) lamp. They accent warm colors like reds, oranges, and yellows, but have a tendency to grey down blues, greens, and cooler hues.

AC (ALTERNATING CURRENT): A flow of electricity that periodically changes its direction; in the U.S. generally, and in most of the world, this change in direction takes place 60 times each second, while in the U.K. it takes place 50 times each second. Other frequencies are used in special applications. Sixty-cycle (now called 60 Hertz) electricity feels the same as the 50-cycle stuff if you touch a wire you ought not to touch. See *DC.*

ACCENT LIGHT: An accent light is a fixture that produces a fairly narrow, controlled beam of light that can be aimed as desired to accent or accentuate a surface or an object.

AMPS (AMPERES): In an electrical circuit, an amp is the unit measuring the amount of electrical current flowing in a conductor. Named for André Marie Ampère (1775–1836).

BAFFLE: A lighting fixture part that prevents light from traveling in a given direction. It is usually used to shield or conceal a bulb or strip light, for example, from certain angles of view—as above a working surface in a kitchen, or in *cornice* or cove lighting.

BALLAST: *Discharge bulbs* such as fluorescent, mercury-vapor, sodium, etc., try to consume ever-increasing amounts of electric current after having been turned on; if they are allowed to do so, they destroy themselves almost instantly. A ballast prevents this from happening by providing the necessary stabilizing characteristics, usually a high voltage for starting the bulb and a lower voltage for running it. The components that do this are usually packaged in a heavy black brick-shaped box with wires coming out of it.

BATTEN: An English term usually applied to a lighting fixture that has the sockets, ballasts, wiring, and structure to hold and run a fluorescent bulb, but has no diffuser, lens, reflector, or anything but the minimum of equipment. In the U.S. it is known as a "bare strip."

BEAM: Any fixture or bulb producing most of its light in a clearly defined direction can be said to be producing a "beam" of light. The beam width or "spread" of the beam is labeled "narrow" (as from a PAR spot bulb), "medium" (as from a PAR flood bulb), or "wide" (as from an R40 flood bulb).

BRIGHTNESS: When we see brightness it is actually light coming from a surface—either reflected, or transmitted, or emitted by a primary source such as the sun or a lamp. For example, a bright coin reflects more light from its surface than a dull one, which has the same area. The importance of defining the term and using it correctly is because when we talk about brightness in relation to lighting equipment we usually mean not how much useful light the fixture produces but how much light comes out from its surfaces and hits you in the eye. When people say things like, "That's a bright light," it is interesting to know whether they mean, "That produces a lot of light" or "That produces a lot of glare."

BULB: The bulb of a lamp is really the glass or quartz enclosure that protects the filament or other light-giving part. But most people use the term for the whole.

CANDELA: This is a term that describes rather confusingly either the unit of intensity of light from a given source *(candle power),* or the unit of brightness of a source when used in terms of area, such as "so many candelas per square inch (or square meter)."

CANDLE: A standard candle, whatever that is, produces 12.57 lumens of light (see *Lumens*) and is still the gentlest and most flattering way of lighting for any number of situations.

CANDLEPOWER: A measure of light intensity. A 150 w. PAR spot bulb for example, has an intensity at the center of its beam of 11,500 candlepower (or candelas) whereas a 150 w. PAR flood bulb has an intensity at the center of its beam of 4,000 candlepower (or candelas).

CHANDELIER: A lighting fixture that has two or more arms or branches, and usually hangs from a ceiling outlet; the term meant originally "candleholder."

CIRCLINE BULB: A fluorescent bulb shaped like a doughnut.

COLOR (IN LIGHTING): The true nature of our perception of color is still being debated. For our purpose, though—which is the understanding and using of light—color is a characteristic not of the surface seen but of the light coming from it. "White" light, from the sun or any other source, is a mixture of red, orange, yellow, green, blue, and violet light. Grass is "green" because it has absorbed all the other colors in the light and reflects only the green. Suppose, choosing a moonless night on which to do it, you shine a red light on a patch of grass. You will see nothing of its "green" because the red light is being absorbed by the green grass and there is no green light in the red beam to be reflected.

COLOR RENDITION: Things look different under bulbs of different colors; how one light source makes, say, skin look, compared to how a different light source might make it look, is the measure of its color-rendering abilities. Bulbs are rated by, among other factors, their "color-rendering index," which takes the form of a number between one and one hundred—the higher the number, the truer the color rendering. However, the numbers are meaningless out of their technical context, or until you have had experience with them. If you want to know which bulb renders colors best for a given purpose, the best way to find out is to try several different kinds for yourself.

COLOR TEMPERATURE: A term for the color of the light source itself, as opposed to the color of the light it produces. Its commonest use is with incandescent photoflash and photoflood bulbs, which are rated so that you will know what film/filter combination to use in your camera. In the case of incandescent bulbs, the color temperature of the source is approximately equal to its true temperature (in degrees Kelvin). In the case of fluorescent and H.I.D. *(high intensity discharge)* bulbs, color temperature is a value arithmetically derived and assigned to the apparent color of the bulb. You cannot use the color temperature of such bulbs as an indicator of their color-rendering properties.

CONTRAST: In lighting, this means principally the contrast between the brightness of an object or surface and the brightness of the background against which that object or surface is seen.

COOL-BEAM BULBS: See *PAR bulbs* for technical information. These are most useful wherever it is desirable to reduce heat from lighting on people and objects, such as in stores, museums, and galleries. The beam of light contains only one-third of the heat (infrared) energy of a conventional PAR bulb of comparable wattage.

COOL WHITE BULB: A fluorescent bulb that is much less flattering than cool white de luxe.

COOL WHITE DE LUXE BULBS: A fluorescent bulb that is inclined to cool down color, so best used in rooms with large amounts of natural light.

CORNICE: For lighting, a shield or baffle, fixed permanently to the ceiling and parallel to the wall. It differs from a *valance* in that a valance is mounted on the wall below the ceiling. Wired and fitted lengths of ready-made cornice are now produced by Lightolier, the American lighting manufacturer. Cornice lighting is simply the downward light coming from equipment installed behind a cornice.

COVE: For lighting, a ledge or shelf on the wall, or a recess in the wall. Cove lighting is upward light thrown from equipment mounted on such a ledge.

DC(DIRECT CURRENT): Electricity flowing in a given direction, as differentiated from alternating current (AC). Incandescent bulbs work equally well with DC or AC, while fluorescent or H.I.D. bulbs, which need ballasts in order to operate, work only on AC. Electricity from a battery is DC, but otherwise one rarely comes across it.

DEGREES KELVIN: A scale used in measuring temperatures, like degrees Fahrenheit and degrees Celsius. In lighting, the term is applied usually to describe the "color temperature" of a bulb. It is named after William Thomson, Baron Kelvin (1824–1907).

DIFFUSER: A device that scatters light from a given source. White *Plexiglas* or *Perspex* is a diffuser and is often used over a fluorescent bulb.

DIMMER SWITCHES: These are essential to any sort of flexible or subtle lighting scheme, since they give a variety of illumination levels at the turn of a knob. There are inexpensive dimmers that fit in place of the usual light switch as well as multiple control units that control several circuits from the same point. There are also separate table-lamp dimmers that can equally well control uplights. They can be operated with fluorescent bulbs (using special ballasts) as well as incandescent or tungsten, and they save energy, bulb life, and running costs. More than worth the money.

DIRECT LIGHTING: Light cast directly onto an object, without reflections from other surfaces such as walls or ceilings.

DISCHARGE BULB: Any bulb in which light is produced by the passage of an electric current through a vapor or gas. Fluorescent, mercury-vapor, metal halide, and high and low pressure sodium are all discharge bulbs of various types; they are generally cheaper to run per lumen of light produced than incandescent light; last longer but are more expensive to buy; and give a less attractive light.

DOWNLIGHT: A lighting fixture that produces all of its light downward; or, light itself directed downward from a lighting fixture.

EARTH: The U.K. equivalent of "ground." See *Grounding.*

EGG-CRATE LOUVER: A set of baffles, intended to shield a bulb from view at certain angles, made from strips of plastic or metal or other material intersecting each other at right angles. Eggs used to be protected by means of cardboard louvers made this way, hence the term.

FITTING(U.K.): English term for *Lighting Fixture.*

FLOOD BULB: A reflector bulb that produces a relatively wide beam of light.

FLUORESCENT BULBS: A tubular bulb coated on the inside with phosphors. They provide different color renderings of "white light," which makes them very different in feeling and rather harsher than the more golden domestic incandescent light. They have the advantage of a very long life—lasting as long as four to five years with normal residential use and normal cleaning care. They are the best lights for energy and money-saving since they cost less to run for each lumen of light produced. Currently, an enormous amount of research is being done on them to make them more acceptable to the domestic market and more flexible. The best color to look for is the Westinghouse Ultralume 3000. "Warm white de luxe" is the next nearest in effect to incandescent light, but the ordinary "cool white" which is the most common actually renders colors rather poorly.

FLUORESCENT TUBE CONTROL GEAR (U.K.): English term for the ballast or for the aggregation of component parts (choke, capacitor, starter, etc.) required to start and run a fluorescent bulb.

FOOT-CANDLE: The (U.S.) measure of the amount of light falling on a given point, which is approximately the total amount of light (1 lumen) thrown onto a surface 1 ft. square and 1 ft. from a candle.

FOOT-LAMBERT: The measure of the amount of light perceived as coming from a surface; i.e. a measure of 1 foot-lambert indicates that 1 lumen of light is being radiated (whether by reflection, transmission, or emission) from each square foot of surface.

FRAMING PROJECTOR: A lighting fixture, the beam of light from which can be shaped so as to fall accurately on an area of a given shape, like a painting or tabletop.

G BULB: A globe-shaped bulb.

GLS BULB: The English equivalent of an American A bulb, the most commonly used bulb shape (see *A Bulb*).

GLARE: Brightness that is undesirable, because it causes annoyance, discomfort, or loss of visual performance.

GROUND FAULT INTERRUPTER: Properly a "ground-fault circuit interrupter"—a device that senses leakage of electric current and breaks the circuit before one can get a shock.

GROUNDING: Establishing a pathway for electricity, in an electrical circuit, through which an abnormal flow of current can be safely diverted (to "ground," or earth) before causing shock or fire. Called *earthing* in the U.K.

H.I.D. (HIGH INTENSITY DISCHARGE) BULB:

A discharge bulb that produces light by means of a high-pressure electric arc passing through a gas vapor like that of mercury. In addition, some H.I.D. lamps produce light by means of a fluorescent coating on the bulb. Although they are most used for industrial purposes, they can be used domestically, for example in outdoor floodlighting for safety and security.

H.P.S. (HIGH PRESSURE SODIUM) BULB: An H.I.D. bulb that produces light by means of a high-pressure electric arc passing through vapor with sodium as its basic constituent. It produces light strong in yellow-pink, but deficient in other colors.

ILLUMINATION: Technically, the level of light (or the number of foot-candles) on a surface.

INCANDESCENT BULB: A bulb producing light simply as a result of having its filament heated to a given temperature by the passage of electricity. The filament is prevented from burning up by being enclosed within a vacuum (as in low-wattage bulbs) or in an atmosphere of inert gases. It is the most common form of domestic lighting and gives a warmer light than fluoresecent. Although fluorescent bulbs are more efficient, incandescent bulbs account for more than half the money spent on domestic lighting in the United States and Great Britain. They are the easiest to install and the least expensive in terms of initial equipment investment.

INDIRECT LIGHTING: Light arriving at a point or surface after reflection from one or more surfaces (usually walls and/or ceilings) which are not part of the lighting fixture.

INTENSITY: The measure of the amount of light (lumens) traveling within a beam of light of a given size or spread. It is usually expressed in *candlepower* or *candelas*.

LENS: Any clear material or combination of clear materials so shaped as to change, by refraction, the path of a ray of light going through it. Commonly used in lighting fixtures both to redirect the light and to conceal the bulb.

LEXAN: Trademark (General Electric Co.) for polycarbonate plastic. It is not as clear as acrylic, and turns yellow as a result of ultraviolet radiation faster than acrylics do, but it is extremely strong, and is the best plastic available for use in lighting fixtures that will be subjected to vandalism or harsh impacts of various kinds (such as stones, baseball bats, etc.). Ideal for street and sports ground fixtures.

LIGHT: Technically, that part of the electromagnetic spectrum to which the eyes respond.

LIGHTING FIXTURE: The ordinary term for the complete unit including the parts that hold and protect the bulb, connect it to its source of electricity, and modify its output. In the U.K. it is called a *fitting* and more technically a *luminaire*.

LINEAR FILAMENT LAMPS: These are the same as strip lights or architectural strips. They are useful above work surfaces, behind baffles, valances, and cornices, and used vertically down the sides of cupboards and alcoves to give warm indirect lighting instead of the equivalent fluorescent tube.

LONG-LIFE BULBS: Long-life bulbs, attractive though they sound, are not the best investment in these energy-conscious days. They *do* last a long time, but at the cost of low efficiency and much wasted energy.

LOUVER: A set of fins or baffles that serve to conceal a bulb and to redirect the light from it. They are commonly made of metal, but can be made of wood, plastic, etc. Architecturally speaking, louvers have their fins all parallel, but in lighting the term is loosely applied, and may mean a square "egg-crate" louver or one made up of hexagons, circles, etc.

LOW-VOLTAGE BULBS: Low-voltage (12 volt) bulbs, with their precise beam control, are used for pinpoint lighting. Some are also designed to cast a rectangular beam for highlighting objects, especially those of a shape similar to the beam. They come in spot and flood forms. When connected to a normal voltage line they must be operated on a transformer. Their actual light is whiter and crisper than standard lighting. They are more expensive to buy than standard equipment, but their cost is offset by their long life.

L.P.S. (LOW-PRESSURE SODIUM) BULB: A bulb that produces light by passing an electric current through vaporized sodium. It is characterized by very high efficiency but also by a yellow light so monochromatic as to render many colors unrecognizable. It is quite often used for street lighting.

LUCITE: Trademark (DuPont Co.) for acrylic plastic.

LUMEN: The unit of quantity of light. The scientific derivation of this measurement is too complicated to explain here, but, for example, a "standard" candle produces about $12^1/_2$ lumens; a new 75 w. incandescent bulb, 1,180 lumens; and a new 40 w. warm white fluorescent bulb, 3,150 lumens.

LUMINAIRE: The technical name for *lighting fixture*.

LUMINANCE: The technical word for *brightness*.

LUMINOUS CEILING: Actually, a translucent ceiling.

LUX: The unit, in the metricated world, expressing the amount of light falling on a given point; equivalent to 1 lumen of light spread over 1 square meter; 10.76 lux equals 1 foot-candle.

MERCURY-VAPOR BULB: An *H.I.D. bulb* that produces light by passing a high-pressure electric arc through mercury vapor. The original clear mercury-vapor bulbs produce a blue-green light unsuitable for a variety of human needs; coated versions, which modify the output and color of the lamp by means of the fluorescing phosphor coating, are somewhat more satisfactory. But before you buy it, try it; and in any case don't use a mercury-vapor bulb inside your house if you care about the appearance of things. Outside, they are good for floodlighting, for safety and security, and, used for suitably wired post lights, they have a very long life. (Note: A ballast is always necessary here.) Low-wattage mercury-vapor bulbs consume up to 60 percent less power than incandescent bulbs of comparable output.

METAL HALIDE BULB: An *H.I.D. bulb* that produces light by means of a high-pressure electric arc passing through a vapor of mercury plus vapors of metallic compounds such as indium thiodide, thallium iodide, etc.

MODELING: In lighting this means to reveal the true form of a three-dimensional object by emphasizing highlights and shadows in an appropriate way—as in good lighting of sculpture.

NEON BULB: A *discharge bulb* in which light is produced by the passage of an electric arc through an atmosphere consisting largely of neon gas. (The light so produced is red; bulbs of other colors, though often referred to as "neon" bulbs, actually use other gases, or are thin fluorescent lamps made with painted or colored-glass tubing.)

PAR BULB: *P*arabolic *A*luminized *R*eflector bulbs having a "punchier" and more dramatic light, with tighter control of beam spread, than an *R bulb.* Their sealed-in reflectors never require cleaning. The 150 w. PAR 38 flood bulb is by far the mose widely used of all the PAR types. The PAR 38 spots are useful where higher intensities are desired. Cool-beam PAR bulbs are bulbs in which the vaporized aluminum inside the reflector has been replaced by a multi-layer of metallic salts. This coating is selective, passing infrared energy or heat through the reflector but reflecting the visible energy or light back into the light beam. They are thus ideal for shops and galleries and wherever it is desirable to reduce radiant heat on people and objects.

PERSPEX: English trade name for methyl methacrylate (acrylic plastic).

PLEXIGLAS: American trademark (Rohm and Haas Company) for methyl methacrylate; also, generically, *plexiglass.*

PLUGMOLD: Trademark of the Wiremold Company. These are strips inset with receptacles onto or into which various fixtures can be clamped or plugged. They can be used around the perimeters of rooms, above baseboards or skirtings, or under platforms and seating to make them appear to float.

POLYCARBONATE: See *Lexan.*

QUARTZ BULB: Commonly but inaccurately used to denote a tungsten-halogen bulb (in which the filament is enclosed in a quartz casing, which has better temperature-resistant qualities than glass does.)

R BULB: A type of reflector bulb. Little R bulbs (General Electric) are very small and ideal for focusing a stream of light toward the precise area needed in fine detail work. These are 25 w., 1 $\frac{3}{4}$ in./44 mm in diameter, with flood distribution.

RECESSED: In lighting, means "built into" an architectural surface such as a ceiling, a wall, even a floor.

REFLECTANCE: Term referring to the amount of light reflected by a given surface compared to the amount of light reaching it. Black paint may have a reflectance of 3 percent, blue of 25 percent, orange of 40 percent, white of up to 90 percent.

REFLECTION: In lighting this means changing the direction of a ray of light by bouncing it off a surface. The angle at which it leaves the surface is equal to the angle at which it hits the surface. Most "background" light is reflected light.

REFLECTOR BULBS: Any of a large family of reflector, or reflectorized, incandescent bulbs, incorporating an internal silver or aluminum coating designed to project light in a given direction. The projected beam of light may be wide (flood) or narrow (spot): the *R* and *PAR* bulbs are the main types, and each has quite different qualities of brilliance, beam spread, etc. To make every watt count, you could replace all 100 w. bulbs in directional fixtures for "task" lights with 50 w. R20 reflector bulbs. You will get about the same amount of light.

REFRACTION: In lighting, the process by which the direction of a ray of light changes as it passes from one medium to another in which its speed is different; for example, as it passes from air into glass and back into air, as in a lens.

RHEOSTAT: An obsolete type of dimmer switch; the name survives.

SEALED-BEAM BULB: Automobiles used to be equipped with lamps positioned in a reflector-lens-socket assembly. This assembly of separate parts evolved into a lamp that integrated the filament, reflector, and lens into one sealed assembly, thus eliminating problems of accurate placement of the filament, dirt on the reflector, etc. It was the forerunner of the common PAR and R bulbs.

SPECULAR REFLECTION: As from a mirror or a polished chrome surface. The opposite would be a diffuse reflection as from a matte white surface.

SPOT BULB: A *reflector bulb* that produces a relatively narrow beam of light.

SPREAD LENS: A lens that spreads light from a lamp evenly across a wall without allowing it to spill into the room. The resulting beam of light is more or less fan-shaped.

T BULB: Any bulb having a tubular configuration; the ordinary fluorescent variety is the most familiar example.

TASK LIGHTING: Lighting providing the illumination for a manual or visual task (sewing, reading) and for the immediate background of the task, but only incidentally, or not at all, for the rest of the space.

THREE-WAY BULBS: Three-way bulbs have two filaments. Each can be operated separately or in combination with the other. It is an excellent energy saver. It can be turned high for reading, writing, or sewing; on the middle setting it can be used for TV viewing, talking, and entertaining; and on the lowest it can be used as a night light or for a subdued atmosphere. Three-way bulbs are generally available from a 30/70/100 w. size to a 100/200/300 one. You need a special three-way socket and switch to take advantage of the three-way effect. Since there are two filaments in the lamp there are two contacts in the base. Tightening the lamp in the socket should ensure that both of these contacts are connected.

TRACK LIGHTING: Track makes it possible for one lighting point to supply a number of separate fittings which can be fitted at any point along its length. It can be surface-mounted or recessed, used in ceilings or on walls, or above baseboards or skirtings, placed vertically or horizontally, singly or in parallels, or in squares, rectangles, or large-diameter circles. It is particularly useful if you do not mind its somewhat technical appearance when there are no ceiling recesses, or not enough outlets. Lightolier of America now produces a miniature track called Lyte Trim with miniature spots for bookshelves, headboards, and cupboards, which can be affixed with a twist of a couple of screws. Low-voltage bulbs need special transformers before they can be used on such a track.

TRANSFORMERS: An instrument that allows the input of one voltage and an output of another.

TRANSLUCENT: Allowing light to pass through; a pigmented, etched, or frosted surface that is not itself see-through.

TRANSMITTANCE: A ratio relating the amount of light going through a material to the amount of light falling on it. Clear glass may have a transmittance of over 95 percent; tinted and colored glass may have a transmittance as low as 5 percent.

TRANSPARENT: Allowing vision through.

TUNGSTEN-HALOGEN BULB: An incandescent bulb having the filament enclosed in an atmosphere that has a certain proportion of special gases known as "halogens"; this produces a longer life, less blackening of the bulb, and a "whiter" light. They give up to 20 percent more light than an equivalent A or GLS bulb. They are expensive and need to be installed with delicacy in order not to damage the outer casing.

UPLIGHT: A canister-shaped lighting fixture that produces all its light upward; or, light itself going upward from a fixture.

VALANCE: A shield or baffle, mounted on the wall well below the ceiling, shielding from view a bulb or lighting fixture installed between it and the wall.

VOLTS: In an electrical circuit, the potential energy available; or, using the water supply system analogy, the pressure waiting to be used. Named for Count Alessandro Volta (1745–1827).

WALLWASHER: A lighting fixture that, when installed in correct relationship to a wall, will light it evenly from top to bottom without spilling or wasting light away from the wall into the room.

WARM WHITE BULB: A fluorescent bulb that belies its name. It is better to use *warm white de luxe* domestically.

WARM WHITE DE LUXE BULB: A fluorescent bulb with color-rendering properties superior to those of the standard *warm white* bulb—therefore better for domestic use.

WATTS: In an electrical circuit, the amount of power being delivered as a result of the flow of a current (in *amps*) multiplied by the pressure of that flow of current (in *volts*). Named after James Watt (1736–1819).

Index

Page references in italic type refer to illustrations.

ABOUT THE AUTHORS

Mary Gilliatt designs interiors and writes articles about interior design—on both sides of the Atlantic. She is design consultant to New Dimension, the British furnishing company, and to Debenham's, one of leading British retailing groups. She has written several books on various facets of design and decor, including *English Style in Interior Decoration; Kitchens and Dining Rooms; Bathrooms; Doing Up a House; A House in the Country; Setting Up Home;* and *Decorating: A Realistic Guide. Decorating* has just been made into a thirteen-part series for British television and is the first series of its kind anywhere.

Douglas Baker, who supplied the technical data for the book, is an experienced lighting designer and consultant, and has designed the lighting for many prize-winning interiors.